D0984657

LESSONS FROM OUR FATHERS

"Hey...Dad?...you wanna have a catch?"

~ Kevin Costner, *Field of Dreams*

One father is more than a hundred schoolmasters.

~ English Proverb

LESSONS FROM OUR FATHERS

KEITH J. McDERMOTT

Printed in the United States of America.

For information address:
Durban House Publishing Company, Inc.
7502 Greenville Avenue, Suite 500, Dallas, Texas 75231

Library of Congress Cataloging-in-Publication Data
McDermott, Keith J., 1960–

Lessons from Our Fathers / by Keith J. McDermott

Library of Congress Catalog Number: 2006923982

p. cm.

ISBN 1-930754-91-4

First Edition

10 9 8 7 6 5 4 3 2 1

Visit our Web site at
http://www.durbanhouse.com

ACKNOWLEDGEMENTS

I have never written a book before. Even now, I am a narrator or compiler, rather than an author. I have no track record, and therefore anyone who agreed to be a part of it was making a leap of faith. The people whose stories appear in this book are famous and successful in their chosen professions, and they all have amazing tales. They provided their time and created openings in their busy schedules to be interviewed or to write a story. I have had the opportunity to thank each of them, but I also want to acknowledge the many people behind the scenes who were instrumental in getting this book to the shelves.

First, I would like to thank all the publicists, corporate communications folks, assistants, students and colleagues of the contributors who listened to my request and passed on the information to the people I wanted to interview. In many cases I was quite a pest, but they handled their jobs as gatekeepers very well and in almost every case were very patient and polite to me. A very special thanks to Eleanor Mascheroni for her help and encouraging words.

After I realized that sending out a truckload of letters was not going to get the access I needed, I decided to enlist and rely on the kindness and aid of friends. They really helped to get the project started. These included Joe Ingrassia, Alanna Kettles, Mike Dunn and his sons, my strong to very strong friends Kevin and Pat, Gene Bay, Beth Beasley, Joe DeLany, Joan Donovan, Beth Barnett, Chris Hardart, Toby Blumenthal, Antoinette and Alicia Kuritz, Martha-Delle Wilson and John Warren. You all were wonderful to help me, and I appreciate your friendship and assistance.

Thank you to John Lewis, Karen Lewis and Bob Middlemiss of Durban House for making my dream become a reality.

There were also many people, like Lee Bradshaw, Katie Meeker, Chris Duhon and Scott Schoenberg, who worked very hard trying to secure some participants. Thanks for the effort.

To my editor, Chuck Perry, thank you – you have made this book much better.

Thanks to my dog, Crash, for sitting at my feet through the entire process, occasionally looking up adoringly and providing the unconditional love pets give.

As I spoke with former United States Presidents, Hall of Fame athletes, university presidents, Nobel Prize winners, corporate titans, and rock 'n' roll stars, I came to realize how much their families, specifically their fathers, helped to shape their lives. The same is true for me. Thank you to my mother, father and brother for the encouragement and positive words. You have always been there for me, and I appreciate you more and more every day.

—Keith J. McDermott

LESSONS FROM OUR FATHERS

TO MOM, DAD, AND STEVE

Table of Contents

INTRODUCTION

On September 11, 2001, I thought I lost my dad.

I was flying back at 6:30 a.m. to my home in Atlanta from Denver, Colorado, after attending the Monday Night Football game between the Denver Broncos and the New York Giants. It was the first week of the NFL season, the grand opening of Invesco Field at Mile High, and it had been a great night spent with good friends – except for my Giants losing. My plane was somewhere over Oklahoma when the pilot came on the PA system and calmly said that we were going to be diverted to Tulsa. Due to a hijacking on the East Coast, all air traffic was to be grounded. I was half asleep at the time and thought very little of it.

When we touched down and were permitted to turn on our cell phones, a cacophony of electronic ringing filled the cabin. Every passenger with a cell phone had a loved one or friend calling to make sure they were safe. The calls were also providing details of the tragic events in New York, Washington and Pennsylvania. I spoke with my girlfriend, who said the words I will never forget: "The Twin Towers are gone."

My father's office was right next to where the World Trade Center stood.

As I gathered my things from the overhead compartment, my mind was in a fog. All I could think of was my father. I had not yet seen any news accounts or pictures, or talked to anyone at home in New York, so worst-case scenarios were flashing through my mind. I tried futilely to reach my father, mother and brother, all of whom were in New York. No calls to Manhattan were going through. I received half a dozen calls in succession from the friends in Colorado I had just left and friends in Atlanta, but they could offer no additional news. I found a television and watched the network accounts. The only picture they were showing was of the vast emptiness, completely enshrouded in dust, which was once the World Trade Center.

I thought he was gone.

The passengers from my plane were hustled onto a series of waiting vans that took us to hotels in downtown Tulsa, where we were to stay until air traffic resumed. Outside the terminal was a gaggle of reporters trying to get a story. One local television crew approached me and a young woman put her microphone in my face, asked me for my opinion on the tragic events of the day and waited for a response. I came close to breaking down and asked her to please speak with someone else because I had family and friends in New York City. She graciously complied.

I finally heard from my brother Steve. He had witnessed the second plane striking the tower from his office window. He was in shock over what had transpired. We both knew people in the Towers, we both had grown up in New York, and we both were worried sick about our father's safety. We began to piece together the events and create a time line that hopefully led to our father's well being. Dad was smart – he would have left and gone uptown as soon as the second plane hit. We were sure.

The next few hours were among the longest of my life. As with many other Americans and men and women from around the world, it was a time of reflection. I mentally took stock of everything that was important to me. I prayed for the victims, for their families that remained and for whom the coming weeks, months and years would be filled with sorrow and loss. I also prayed to hear from my dad.

And my prayers were answered. I felt like I had been given a second chance.

He had been uptown at a meeting when the terrorists attacked and was alive and well. He may not understand to this day what it was like for me to hear his voice. He may not know that I had tears in my eyes on the other end of the line as I sat on that bed in a downtown Tulsa hotel. He may not relate to how relieved I was when I heard he was safe at home with my mother. But I know he remembers that I told him I loved him and how happy I was that he was all right. After the five or six hours of not knowing, the worrying and being unsure, it was a happy moment during a very sad time.

My father was born on February 3, 1929, which makes him 77 years young as this book is published. He still works. In fact, he got a new job when he was 70 years old. And not only did he uproot himself from a nice, midtown New York City office within walking distance of the train he took every morning and move downtown, but he convinced his entire division to come with him. You see, my father was being squeezed by a couple of his partners; they thought they could push the old guy around. So he took his clients, their hundreds of millions of dollars, his co-workers and his experience and found a place where he was shown respect. I was so proud of him!

But that is my dad, always tenacious, always hard working and not someone to be pushed around–especially when he is right. He was born and raised in the Bronx and, although he is considered a well-spoken, highly educated and polished man, there is a certain degree of urban toughness that remains. My father has taught me many lessons. I have tried to learn by his example and tried to emulate him and the way he lives his life. He is a devoted husband to my mother, Jean, whom he has been married to for 45 years. He is one of the most honest people I have ever met, and he trained me to realize right from wrong. He never misses church. He has a great sense of humor and a true gift for story telling (even though we may have heard some of them a few hundred times!). He has exercised his entire life and continues to run, lift weights and play all sorts of racquet sports in order to stay physically fit. He poured body and soul into another great love of his life, The New York Athletic Club, where he served as president in the late '80s and where he still sits on a number of committees. He is a voracious reader. He has donated a tremendous amount of time and money to various charities and to his alma maters, Fordham Preparatory School, Fordham University, and Fordham Law School (it is safe to call him a Fordham man). I cannot remember a football, baseball or basketball game of mine all the way through high school that he did not attend. The same goes for my brother Steve and all his games. Dad was always there, and I always remember his fist pumping and his mouthing words of encouragement from the stands to me on the field, court or sidelines. Although the sandlots of high school and college have given way to the playing field of real life, he has continued to provide counsel and support for me. I always turn first to him.

He is truly my best friend, and I am lucky to call him Dad.

As you read this book, you will find that the people who provided the stories of their relationships with their fathers feel much the same way. Their love and respect for the fathers who raised them certainly was apparent to me, and I hope it shines through the text as you read it. The book is filled with life lessons, funny anecdotes, a few sad stories and even a little bit of mysticism. But overall, it is a study in the wisdom and lessons that have been imparted by fathers to this very special group of people.

FOREWORD

Our world has suffered mightily from the perverse hoax that kids don't need to have fathers (and the cruel corollary that men needn't experience fathering themselves to give their lives meaning, i.e., to connect themselves to the past and the future of the human race and make themselves part of something bigger than themselves). This book gives those hoaxes the lie and instead reveals fifty-one very similar opnions from fifty-one very different people about what it takes to be a successful father.

The intrepid Keith McDermott has pulled together fifty-one celebrated contributors who share two things: they have all achieved greatness and they all give much of the credit to their fathers — fifty-one successful fathers who were usually there, at home with the family. Even when they were not at home, but were off at work or at war, they were always committed and connected, always working for the family or for the world. These fathers we love and recall so adoringly were not off on the golf course and they did not run off with the neighbor lady. First and foremost they were fathers, trying to pass on to their children whatever skills they had and whatever they had learned of the secrets of the universe, the wisdom and understanding of the way the world works and the way their sons and daughters can get through life in one piece and with their heads held high.

The advice fathers pass on to their children may be the depth of wisdon, or it may be off the wall. It doesn't really matter, since the important thing fathers do is be there. I have to recall the most memorable piece of advice my father gave me, when I was 16 and had rushed home to tell him of an appaling experience I'd just had: getting shot at. I needed a man's advice in the matter and he was there for me. He reached down into his store of wisdom and wisely intoned: "Son, only a fool would ever drink homemade whiskey with a tattooed lady hitchhiker." Actually, I hadn't heard that particular lesson before, and I've never crossed that line since. My father's wisdom was often surprising. On that occasion, his advice, however wise, was hardly brilliant, but his presence, his calm practicality and his humor about the situation were glorious.

I believe *Lessons from Our Fathers* captures what it takes to be a successful father as well as anything I've read. These sons and daughters may respect or even be awed by the accomplishments of their fathers, but mostly they come alive in the moments or decades of connection with their fathers. In that connection, they shape an identity as an adult, they receive the paternal anointment that welcomes them into the larger world, and they reciprocate his welcome.

The contributors here tell us that the most important thing fathers can do is not to give advice, but to be there—in person or in spirit or in memory. For the few children of divorce in the collection, like Michael Reagan and Christie Hefner, the parental divorce was the central crisis that shaped their lives, and they grew up valuing those things their fathers valued.

Generatons of fathers, not knowing what fathers are for, try to do it efficiently or even competitively, as they would a sport or a job. They may try to make starker differentiations between what a man does as a father from what a woman does as a mother. They may try to do whatever they do in "quality time" when fathering really requires "quantity time," a man and a child side by side as the man not only lets the child see life through a father's eyes, but lets the child hear, smell and feel what it is like to be a man.

This book answers the basic post-Freudian question: what are men for anyway? Women can, of course, do whatever a man can do, can even be Pope, President. The only thing a man can do that a women can't is be a father. He doesn't have to be strong or wise or right, or win one of life's many symbolic or real contests, he just needs to be there, showing by his presence that he values his child and his child's family.

— *Frank Pittman, internationally*
acclaimed author and psychiatrist

SPECIAL THANKS

As you start reading this book, your first reaction upon turning to the first chapter may be one of surprise. You probably noticed on the cover or in the index that there are stories about their fathers from former Presidents, leaders of civil rights movements, business leaders, rock stars and famous actors. You may wonder why – in a group of people with so many accomplishments on such a grand scale – I would choose to start with a golfer, albeit one of the most recognizable and respected athletes of the last century. It is because he believed in me and in this project.

When I first began to pursue my idea for this book, I wrote letters to people in all walks of life, thinking that getting a good response would be a piece of cake. I felt that it was such a noble pursuit with great intentions that anyone who had a strong relationship with his or her father would want to be involved. How could the great politicians, scholars, entertainers, religious leaders, educators and so forth not want to tell of their upbringing and provide an anecdote or some advice that their dear old dad had imparted to them?

But no one seemed to care.

After spending the better part of two months sending out letters, each with a self-addressed, stamped envelope, I heard from a few publicists or agents' assistants with form letters saying their client would not be interested in contributing or being interviewed. From close to four hundred letters I sent out, I received approximately 50 responses.

I received exactly one response from an individual saying he was interested in contributing to my book. He had provided a story *and* a wonderful picture with his father.

That response came from Arnold Palmer.

Palmer gave me the motivation to complete my work, despite the slow start, because he had been a hero of mine for as long as I could remember. He exudes class and sportsmanship. He is a winner, he is intelligent, and he is a living legend. I figured that if he thought it was a good idea, and if I worked hard, my dream could become a reality. (Not to mention the fact that I now had Arnold Palmer on board when I asked other people to be a part of the project!)

The story that Palmer sent is about a lesson he learned from his father as a young man. It is simple and yet has seemed to guide him through his life on the world's stage. It also helped to motivate me while undertaking the most meaningful and important task of my life thus far.

I hope you enjoy Arnold Palmer's story and the rest of the stories in *Lessons From Our Fathers*.

—Keith J. McDermott

ARNOLD PALMER

ARNOLD PALMER is one of the most successful athletes of the last 50 years. He is a world-famous golfer, tremendously successful businessman, spokesman and aviator.

His popularity and success have paralleled the tremendous growth and popularity of golf in the last half century. In fact, he presides over the largest non-uniformed "military" organization in existence – Arnie's Army.

Palmer amassed 92 championships in professional competition of national or international stature by the end of 1993. Sixty-one of the victories came on the U.S. PGA Tour, starting with the 1955 Canadian Open.

Seven of his victories came in what the golfing world considers the four major professional championships. He won the Masters tournament four times (1958, 1960, 1962 and 1964); the U.S. Open in spectacular fashion in 1960 at Cherry Hills Country Club in Denver; and the British Open in 1961 and 1962. He came from seven strokes behind in the final round of that U.S. Open win, and he finished second in four other Opens. Among the majors, only the PGA Championship has eluded him. He finished second in the PGA three times.

Palmer was born on September 10, 1929, in Latrobe, a small

industrial town in Western Pennsylvania at the foothills of the Allegheny Mountains some 50 miles east of Pittsburgh. He still spends the warm months of the year there but makes his winter home in the Orlando area.

The golfing great has been the recipient of countless honors, many reflected in plaques, trophies and citations that fill the walls of his offices. He has received virtually every national award in golf, including the Hickok Athlete of the Year and *Sports Illustrated*'s Sportsman of the Year for 1960. He is a charter member of the World Golf Hall of Fame and the American Golf Hall of Fame at Foxburg, PA, and the PGA Hall of Fame in Florida.

He also gives much time to charity work and served as Honorary National Chairman of the March of Dimes Birth Defects Foundation for 20 years.

Palmer was married to the late Winnie Palmer for nearly 50 years. They were married shortly after he turned professional in the fall of 1954. The Palmers have two daughters, five granddaughters and two grandsons.

Both my parents were on hand to watch my match in the West Penn junior finals. Frustrated at having missed a short putt, I turned and threw my putter in disgust over the gallery and some small trees. My elation at winning quickly vanished when I was greeted with dead stone silence in the family car. "If you ever throw a club like that again," my father told me, barely restraining his fury, "you'll never play in another golf tournament."

I know my father was brimming with pride, but I'd violated one of his cardinal rules about life and golf – that learning to be a gracious loser is at least as important as being a gracious winner. Being an ungracious winner was perhaps the worst thing he could imagine.

I was enough like my mother, I guess, that I was incapable of hiding my emotions at either winning or losing. But thanks to Pop, I learned the value of never publicly displaying my frustration – frustration every golfer experiences – and keeping my emotions in a bottle when I lost regardless of the depth of disappointment, of which there would be plenty. More to the point, I never threw a club like that in anger again.

LAMAR ALEXANDER

LAMAR ALEXANDER was born in Maryville, Tennessee, the son of a kindergarten teacher and elementary school principal. He is a seventh generation Tennessean.

He has been governor of the state (1979-1987), president of the University of Tennessee (1988-1991) and United States Education Secretary (1991-1993). In private life, he helped found a company that is now the nation's largest provider of work-site day care. He taught about the American character as a faculty member at Harvard's School of Government. In 2002, he won election to the U.S. Senate, the first Tennessean to be popularly elected both governor and senator.

In his campaign for governor, Lamar Alexander walked 1,000 miles across Tennessee and, once elected, he helped Tennessee become the third largest auto producer, the first state to pay teachers more for teaching well and the fastest growing state in family incomes.

He is a classical and country pianist and the author of seven books, including *Six Months Off*, the story of his family's life in Australia after he was governor.

He is married to the former Honey Buhler of Victoria, Texas. They have four children.

Lamar Alexander's father, Andy, started the ball rolling for his son. He enjoyed music immensely – and his son became a classical pianist. He dabbled in local politics – and his son became both governor and U.S. Senator from his home state. Early in his career, he worked as an elementary school principal – and his son has focused on education as his primary issue during his time in government.

"My dad was born in 1907 on a farm south of Maryville, Tennessee, on the Little Tennessee River. He originally served as a teacher at Westside Elementary School in Maryville. During the Depression in the 1930s, he attended Maryville College, and because he had to work and earn money, it took him a few extra years to graduate. He was well liked, and a close friend told me once, 'Everybody always liked to see Andy coming.'

"By the time I came along he was the principal, but then he was offered a job that paid twice as much at the Aluminum Company of America (ALCOA) plant. He worked there for the rest of his career as the director of safety, but he continued his interest in education.

"He and a group of four others in Maryville ran for the school board after World War II on the same ticket. They all got elected and their goal was to transform the school system and make it better. They hired a professional superintendent for the school system and they stayed there, the five of them, for twenty-five years. Today it's the school system that year-in and year-out has the top academics and test scores in the state.

"He was a member of the Republican Executive Committee for the county and was very active in the Boy Scouts, where he was awarded the Silver Beaver Award for his work.

"He passed on a great passion for music to me. He had a beautiful tenor voice and sang quartet while in college. He also had an uncle, Charles M. Alexander, who at the beginning of the 20th century was the Cliff Barrows (Billy Graham's song leader) of his era. In fact, Cliff Barrows himself told me that Charles M. Alexander was his inspiration in life and showed him what it was that he wanted to do.

Sometimes when I was a young boy, he would lead the singing and I would play piano at church meetings.

"He identified a Bible verse whenever he would sign his name – 2 Timothy 2:15: 'Study to show thyself approved unto God, a workman that needeth not to be ashamed, rightly dividing the word of truth.'

"That was always my dad's favorite verse, and it was the verse to which the Bible was opened when I was sworn in as governor in 1979, re-elected in 1982, and then again when I was sworn in as senator on the same family Bible.

"When I was ten, my father took me to the Blount County Courthouse to meet our congressman one Saturday morning, and I never forgot it. It was a major occasion. The congressman gave me a dime and shook my hand, and I was sure when I left that this was the most respected man I was ever likely to meet, other than my father and the preacher. It was that sort of respect for public officials and public life at an early age that undoubtedly created in me the kind of respect that I have for our system of government and democracy. That congressman's name was Howard Baker, Sr.

So a few years later, when Congressman Baker's son ran for U.S. Senate in 1966, I volunteered for his campaign, went to Washington with him as his legislative assistant, and I serve in the same seat today that he served in 1966. Actually, we have the same telephone number. My father's example and the respect he taught me – both by serving on the school board and making time for the Republican Executive Committee and going down on election night to count votes, and the fact that he thought it was important to take me to the courthouse to introduce me to Congressman Baker – made a big difference to me and greatly influenced what I do today.

JUDGE GRIFFIN B. BELL

GRIFFIN BELL was appointed by President Jimmy Carter and served as the 72nd Attorney General of the United States from 1977-79. In 1961, President John F. Kennedy appointed him to serve as a United States Circuit Judge on the Fifth Circuit Court of Appeals. Judge Bell served on the Fifth Circuit for 15 years until 1976, when he returned to the law firm of King & Spalding in Atlanta, Georgia.

He is a member of the American College of Trial Lawyers, serving as its president from 1985-86. He is also a member of the American Law Institute.

Judge Bell was the initial Chairman of the Atlanta Commission on Crime and Juvenile Delinquency. During 1980, he headed the American delegation to the conference on Security and Cooperation in Europe, held in Madrid. In 1984, Judge Bell received the Thomas Jefferson Memorial Foundation Award for Excellence in Law. From 1985-87, he served on the Secretary of State's Advisory Committee on South Africa, and in 1989 he was appointed vice chairman of President Bush's Commission on Federal Ethics Law Reform. During the Iran Contra investigation, he was counsel to President G.H.W. Bush.

Judge Bell graduated *cum laude* from Mercer University Law School in 1948.

My father grew up on a farm in southwest Georgia and was a cotton farmer until the boll weevil came and he had to stop. I get my hard working inclination from him. He had a lot of sayings like, "Make yourself useful," and "Find *something* to do." They had a marked influence on me.

When I was a small boy, he started talking to me about being a lawyer. He wanted me to practice law. He used to take me by the courthouse to let me watch trials when court was in session in Americus, Georgia. He had a cousin who was a lawyer who was actually made Chief Justice of the Georgia Supreme Court, and he tried to pattern me to take after him. Turned out I did.

My father was able to see me take the bench, and he held the Bible in 1961 when I was sworn in. It was a big day. He was very proud of the fact that I became a judge and even told me that was his dream.

He was a very kind man and had a good sense of caring for other people, and I think I learned that from him. He thought a lot about community and helping others and also passed on his interest in politics. He was a city councilman and chairman of the county Democratic Party. He kept up with what was going on and all the issues. He was the first person who ever told me about term limits. He thought it was a bad thing to keep people in office too long. He wanted to change that.

My son is a lawyer now, too. I tried to take the same approach with him that my father took with me. I have good relations with him and at first he did not much want to enter the law. He wanted to be a history teacher. After he served in Vietnam, he changed his mind. During his service they put him on Court Martials, and they had him doing some representation. He liked it and enjoyed it and wrote me a letter asking for an application to Emory Law School, and he started as soon as he got home. My father's passion that was transferred to me had made its way to my son. I was very pleased.

My father would have made a good lawyer because he was very

good with people. He did not argue so much, but he presented the facts very well and used good judgment. He taught me that sometimes it pays to be the calm one, especially in a courtroom.

He was a history buff and he passed that on to me, and it is very helpful, especially in politics and government, to know the past. Even in today's climate, with regards to military trials and the war on terror, a lot of people do not seem to understand that this is an old procedure, not a new one. We have had military trials since the Revolutionary War. The only thing that is different is that now we are not fighting a country. We are fighting an enemy, but they do not have a country.

I had a lot of experience when I was in the government with foreign intelligence. So being a history buff, I read up on the military trials of World War II, one of which took place at the Justice Department in the office next to the Attorney General's office. The case involved German spies and submarines, and it was all very intriguing but also precedent for things that went on during my tenure and also today. Knowing history cannot be underestimated.

JOHN BELL

JOHN BELL was born April 14, 1962, in Cleveland, Ohio, and is the leader, guitarist and vocalist of the rock 'n' roll band Widespread Panic. The band's long voyage began in the mid-80s with some friends getting together to make music while attending college at the University of Georgia in Athens. Playing for parties led to paying gigs at fraternity houses and bars, and eventually the word spread far enough to justify taking to the road and visiting other southeastern locales.

Success has not been a meteoric rise. There were years when the band would play 250 dates per year and be traveling almost constantly. It was a life of cheap hotels, half-empty bars and fast food. But the hard work and grassroots marketing paid off. Along with bands like Phish and the Dave Matthews Band, Widespread Panic is at the forefront of the "jam band" genre that has followed, emulated and evolved from a concept originally fashioned by bands such as The Grateful Dead.

To date the band has recorded eight studio albums and released a number of live recordings. In 1998 they returned home to Athens, where they played a free concert to celebrate the release of the album *Light Fuse, Get Away.* More than 100,000 of their close friends showed up, essentially taking over the town and stretching as far as the eye could see.

In recent years the band has headlined the Bonnaroo Music

Festival, a celebration of the jam band style and appeared on both *The Late Show with David Letterman* and *The Tonight Show with Jay Leno.* A full-length documentary on the band, *The Earth Will Swallow You,* was released in theaters in 2002 and became a nationwide bestseller after being released on DVD. At the end of 2003, Widespread Panic performed two sold-out shows at "the world's most famous arena," Madison Square Garden in New York City.

Dad and I had just started out for a "walk around the block" one fall evening when I was about four or five years old. Suddenly a rush of leaves chased after an ambulance as it sped by. I had been anticipating the jingle of an ice cream truck, but at that moment, I grabbed my ears to escape the sound of an invading siren. My father's words slipped between my fingers and into memory.

"You know what I do when I hear an ambulance, Johnny? I wish that person inside good luck."

With that simple communication, this little guy from Ohio was struck by the realization that every person was as alive as we are, and those lives are important, even if we may never meet them. Ever since that evening, when I hear a siren, I imagine the faces of families I may not know (cats and dogs included) and I wish them good luck.

A few years later, Dad and my mom were hanging out on the front step of our house, which faced the large playground and recreation area of my elementary school. Some of the older boys were on their bikes racing home. In the growing shadows, the kids didn't notice that a chain had been stretched across the fence opening. The boy in the lead hit the chain with his front wheel, flew off the bicycle seat onto the blacktop and knocked out two of his front teeth. My parents ran across the street, picked up his teeth, found out where he lived and delivered him home to his folks. These days, playground dangers come in much more complicated forms than was the case in the '60s, but I knew then that my mom and dad felt it was their responsibility to take care of this boy, and they acted without hesitation. It was real life, not TV, and I thought that was very cool.

Being part of a touring rock 'n' roll band for almost 20 years has provided a great deal of surprises – sometimes scary ones. I can't help thinking that my parents' example in both action and advice, in my earliest years, plays a huge role in my ability to keep my wits more or less intact on those occasions. Wishing someone luck is a good thing, but in taking it upon yourself to help out, you can become an active component of good fortune.

My father had some early, wonderfully positive training as well. The tone in his voice reveals his pride when he talks about his own father. Dr. James R. Bell, Sr., served in World War II as chief of medicine with Air Transport Command in Newfoundland. My grandfather specialized in internal medicine, continuing to practice well into his eighties. He maintained life-long relationships with patients of limited financial resources, and he made house calls to friends and neighbors, including those more in need of human attention than medical care.

As long as I can remember, Dad expressed his admiration for family members, living and ancestral. He has uncovered and shares many facts and stories that may have otherwise gone forgotten.

The summer after one of my junior years in college, Dad and I made our way up to New England to search through small town records and burial grounds for information pertaining to the family lineage. We found an unmarked dirt road we didn't know we were looking for. While examining our map, we happened to meet the adopted son of a related Bell. The man hopped off his tractor, jumped a ditch, met us at the car window and fairly questioned, "What are you folks doin'... way out here?" Intrigued by a possible family connection, he jumped into the back seat, joining us for the day as a scout for relocated Scots-Irish. We found written records on many great, great, great relations in the Massachusetts and New Hampshire areas, but reading the headstones of the first couple to cross the Atlantic really stays with me. James and Martha Bell landed in their new land around 1707, at ages of seven and eight, and both lived to be 87 years old. They had eight children; among them doctors, carpenters, and westbound settlers.

I don't know if it was his intention, but my father left me with a sense of wonder; where do I fit in with this family? What am I going to do? Who am I going to be as I continue to grow up?

Now I'm a musician, although I consider myself more as a band member. Dad didn't lead me to this career aside from letting me discover my own way. He set me up with piano and guitar lessons, but he let me opt out when he saw that I'd rather be at the playground. My folks bought my brother a guitar that I inherited at age nine. Pop would knock on my bedroom wall and ask me to come witness musicians performing miracles on the Johnny Carson show. He firmly encouraged me to purchase my own set of golf clubs when he had increasing trouble finding his own. I was presented with all kinds of opportunities. I never remember feeling pushed in any direction, musical or otherwise. However, through my father, I was acquiring a sense of the importance of simple awareness – consideration of others, taking in my surroundings and learning the wonder of history and possibility.

James Roeder Bell, Jr., was raised in Shaker Heights, Ohio. He graduated Harvard University and Harvard Business School. An investment banker, my father became self-employed in the mid '60s, still lending his talents to research and development of new systems and inventions. In the early '70s, Dad's friend, Jim Fergason, explained that he was onto something that was to be "*the* major interface between electronics and the human eye." Through their partnership and research, the liquid crystal display (or LCD) by which we tell time, watch TV and read e-mail today was born. Once in a while Pop would bring home models that demonstrated the various stages of development of liquid crystal displays. For four years, I was the "King of Show and Tell."

Currently my father is working with researchers at Case Western Reserve Medical School in Cleveland, discovering new lines of attack against autoimmune diseases. I get caught up in his excitement as he describes the processes and relationships within and beyond the scientific realm – feels like jazz. I am so proud of him.

One opinion my father shared that might best tie together this small batch of memories: he said, "Johnny, if you had the opportunity to hear everybody's story, all of what they'd been through in life, those would be the stories of heroes."

Everybody can be a hero. Some may already be there and not know it.

Thank you, Pop, for my ongoing lessons.

CATHLEEN BLACK

CATHLEEN BLACK is president of Hearst Magazines, a division of The Hearst Corporation and one of the world's largest publishers of monthly magazines. She oversees the financial performance and development of some of the industry's best-known titles: *Cosmopolitan*; *Esquire*; *Good Housekeeping*; *Harper's BAZAAR*; *Marie Claire*; *O, The Oprah Magazine*; *Popular Mechanics*; *Redbook*; and *Town & Country* – 18 magazines in all. She also oversees 110 international editions of those magazines in 100 countries.

Having begun her career in advertising sales with several magazines, she made publishing history in 1979 when she became the first woman publisher of a weekly consumer magazine, *New York*.

Black is widely credited for the success of *USA Today,* where for eight years she was first president, then publisher, as well as a board member and executive vice president/marketing of Gannett, its parent company.

She serves as a member of the boards of IBM, iVillage and the Coca-Cola Company, and she recently completed a two-year term as Chairman of the Magazine Publishers of America. She is also a board member of the Advertising Council and a trustee of the University of Notre Dame and The Kent School, Kent, Connecticut.

She has consistently been listed among *Fortune* magazine's "Most Powerful Women in American Business," achieving this honor again in

2003. In 2000, she was named "Publishing Executive of the Year" by *Advertising Age*, and in June 2002, *Crain's New York Business* named her one of its "100 Most Influential Business Leaders."

Black is a graduate of Trinity College, Washington, D.C., and holds eight honorary degrees.

As a young girl, I felt an affinity for my father – we talked a lot. I was always interested in hearing his business stories, and because I found them interesting, we would sit up in the evenings on the front porch of our house in Chicago and I would listen to his business day. I always found it fascinating. Most kids would have had no interest in the subject, but I did. My business interests – although he was not involved in the same industry – were instilled by him.

My mother never worked outside the home. She was a very sharp woman, extremely smart and terrifically funny. She is definitely remembered for her sense of humor. She lived more of a country club existence, and I remember saying to her at a young age, in my early twenties, "I do not know exactly what I want, but I want it to be exciting and be more than the life that you have led." It was probably a little offensive, as I look back on it, using that kind of language, but I did it.

My father instilled in me a desire to succeed and be the best that I could be. I never felt any restrictions from him about what girls could do and not do. I remember talking with him about colleges (after going to a parochial high school that was literally and figuratively parochial in its thinking). A lot of girls were going to Chicago area schools or Midwestern schools, and I mentioned to my father that I wanted to attend a small, Catholic college in Iowa. He looked at me and said, "You know, Cathie, the world is much too big a place for you to go to college in Iowa. Now, there is nothing wrong with going to college in Iowa, but you should think of things on a broader level." So I ended up applying to several schools on the East Coast, finally choosing Trinity College in Washington, D.C. He always encouraged me to dream a big dream and to see life on a bigger playing field. I think for a lot of women of my generation, fathers did not necessarily tell their daughters they could be President of the United States or CEO of US Steel, but I know my father helped me set high goals.

As I approached my junior year in college, my parents did something that was so unselfish. I wanted to spend my junior year abroad and both my parents were very supportive of the decision. As we discussed in my sophomore year whether I should go for a semester or a whole year, he said, “If you are going that far, the best thing is to stay for the entire time.” This came from a man who had never been to Europe, who, with my mother, had traveled in the United States and was relatively sophisticated but had never been abroad. He told me, “You will probably make many new friendships, you will start traveling and will start to enjoy the experience of living in Rome, and I am sure you are not going to want to come home in January.” That was just one of a series of events which he encouraged that allowed my wings to spread.

But it was what happened next that really proved his devotion to me and his own courage. Shortly before I was scheduled to leave in August, my mother had a very bad accident, hit her head and came very close to dying due to blood loss. She and I had many conversations during her recovery about whether I should still go. She was not as encouraging as my father, who still said, “Sweetie, you are only 19 years of age once and you have to live your life. You cannot hold yourself back because of this very difficult period. You should go.”

It was a very giving moment because most people, my parents' friends included, thought that I should probably not go to Rome and should take the semester off to stay at home to help with my mother's recovery.

This was mostly due to the fact that my father was blind.

But he never wanted his blindness to stand in the way, regarding me or anything else. He was a very proud man who tried to function as normally as possible. He had a driver for many years because of the progression of his blindness. And although he refused to use a seeing-eye dog, he used a cane, but not a blind person's cane. He was adamant about being as regular as he could be.

My father was a big personality, and people liked him. He was jovial and smart, just one of those kinds of people who fills the room, in a good way, when they walk in. And he was kind.

He died of a heart attack at age 63, and that was a big loss for me. He never was able to enjoy the successes I have achieved in my personal life and career. But I owe a lot of those accomplishments to him, because deep within me has always been a sense of adventure and a wanting to see the world that I learned from him. He loved his family, and he would love the fact that I went on to marry and have two children. That would be the most important thing to him.

WILLIAM F. BUCKLEY, JR.

WILLIAM F. BUCKLEY, JR., is a "national institution," or so says the *Chicago Tribune*. He has been the intellectual and emotional architect of the American conservative movement since his founding of *National Review* in 1955. After entering the military shortly before the end of World War II, he attended Yale and graduated with honors in 1950. His entrance onto the national literary scene occurred after he penned the hypercritical *God and Man at Yale* about his alma mater. He has won the Presidential Medal of Freedom, an American Book Award and an Emmy for his work on "Firing Line," where guests included everyone from Groucho Marx to His Holiness the Dalai Lama. He has written more than 40 books and has contributed articles to an amazingly eclectic variety of American publications, including *Architectural Digest, Playboy, The New Yorker, The Saturday Evening Post* and *Yachting*. Born in New York City in 1925, the sixth of ten children, Buckley spent his early years in Connecticut, England and France. He and his wife, Patricia, have been married for more than 50 years and have one son, Christopher.

William F. Buckley, Jr., took more from his father than a name. His father was a great statesman and political thinker whose counsel was sought on some of the great dilemmas of his day. "Those who knew him then remember keenly the intelligence, the wit, the large-heartedness and – always – the high principle which brought him a singular eminence in the community," Buckley remembers.

"That eminence the American government repeatedly acknowledged, as when three successive Secretaries of State called on him for guidance; as when the Wilson administration offered him the civil governorship of Vera Cruz (he refused indignantly); as when the Mexican government appointed him counsel at the ABC Conference in Niagra; as when he was called by the Senate Foreign Relations Committee as the premier American expert on the tangled affairs of Mexico. And in 1921, the end of the line: exile from Mexico. For that he was lucky. For he had indeed materially aided a counterrevolutionary movement. The fact that the counterrevolutionists were decent men, and those in power barbarians, does not alter the political reality, which is that it is a very dangerous business indeed to back an unsuccessful insurrection: and he knew it, and barely escaped with his skin."

As leader of the conservative revolution in America, the younger Buckley's literal skin was safe, although he has constantly been the bane of counter-thinkers' existence and the target of their attacks.

But William, Sr., was a man of family as well as a man of government and policy. "He married and had ten children who survived him," his son says, recounting his siblings. "He launched a business in Venezuela, and his fortunes fluctuated. But as children we were never aware of his tribulations. We knew only that the world revolved about him, and that whether what was needed was a bicycle or an excuse to stay away from school for a day, or the answer to an anguished personal problem, he was there to fill the need. And when he thought the need exorbitant or improper, he would, by a word, bring us gently to earth. He worshipped three earthly things: learning, beauty and his family. He satisfied his lust for the first by reading widely, and by imposing on his lawless brood an unusual pedagogical regimen. The second impulse he gratified by a meticulous attention to every shrub, every stick of furniture that composed his two incomparable homes.

The third he served by a constant, inexplicit tenderness to his wife and children, of which the many who witnessed it have not, they say, often seen the like.

In his anxiety for the well-being of his country, his three passions fused. Here in America was the beauty, the abundance, that he revered; here in the political order was the fruit of centuries of learning; here his wife and his ten children, and his 31 grandchildren, would live, as long as he lived, and years after. So he encouraged us to stand by our countries and our principles. To his encouragement, moral and material, *National Review* owes its birth and early life. Two weeks before his death, crippled and convalescent in Austria, he registered, in turn, joy, and indignation, and amusement, and sadness, as his wife read aloud to him from the magazine of his America's glories and misadventures."

William F. Buckley, Jr., like his father before him, has lived life as a patriot, a family man and, in every respect, to the fullest.

PRESIDENT GEORGE H.W. BUSH

GEORGE HERBERT WALKER BUSH, the 41st President of the United States, was born in Milton, Massachusetts, on June 12, 1924.

On his eighteenth birthday, after graduating from Phillips Academy in Andover, he enlisted in the armed forces. The youngest pilot in the Navy when he received his wings, he flew 58 combat missions during World War II. On one mission over the Pacific as a torpedo bomber pilot, he was shot down by Japanese antiaircraft fire and was rescued from the water by a U.S. submarine. He was awarded the Distinguished Flying Cross for bravery in action.

Bush next turned his energies toward completing his education and raising a family. In January 1945 he married Barbara Pierce. They had six children – George, Robin (who died as a child), John (known as Jeb), Neil, Marvin and Dorothy.

At Yale University he excelled both in sports and in his studies; he was captain of the baseball team and a member of Phi Beta Kappa. After graduation Bush embarked on a career in the oil industry of west Texas.

Like his father, Prescott Bush, who was elected a senator from Connecticut in 1952, George became interested in public service and politics. He served two terms as a Representative to Congress from Texas. Twice he ran unsuccessfully for the Senate. Then he was appointed to a series of high-level positions: Ambassador to the United

Nations, Chairman of the Republican National Committee, Chief of the U. S. Liaison Office in the People's Republic of China and Director of the Central Intelligence Agency.

In 1980 Bush campaigned for the Republican nomination for President. He lost but was chosen as a running mate by Ronald Reagan. As Vice President, Bush had responsibility in several domestic areas, including federal deregulation and anti-drug programs, and he visited scores of foreign countries.

In 1988 Bush won the Republican nomination for President and, with Senator Dan Quayle of Indiana as his running mate, defeated Massachusetts Governor Michael Dukakis in the general election.

Bush faced a dramatically changing world, as the Cold War ended after 40 bitter years, the Communist empire broke up and the Berlin Wall fell. The Soviet Union ceased to exist; and reformist President Mikhail Gorbachev, whom Bush had supported, resigned. While Bush hailed the march of democracy, he insisted on restraint in U.S. policy toward the group of new nations.

In other areas of foreign policy, President Bush sent American troops into Panama to overthrow the corrupt regime of General Manuel Noriega, who was threatening the security of the canal and Americans living there. Noriega was brought to the United States for trial as a drug trafficker.

Bush's greatest test came when Iraqi President Saddam Hussein invaded Kuwait, then threatened to move into Saudi Arabia. Vowing to free Kuwait, Bush rallied the United Nations, the U.S. people and Congress and sent 425,000 American troops. They were joined by 118,000 troops from allied nations. After weeks of air and missile bombardment, the 100-hour land battle dubbed "Desert Storm" routed Iraq's million-man army.

Despite unprecedented popularity from this military and diplomatic triumph, Bush was unable to withstand discontent at home from a faltering economy, rising violence in inner cities and continued high deficit spending. In 1992 he lost his bid for reelection to Democrat Bill Clinton.

I married someone who shared the same ideals of breaking away from the family and making it on my own. Barbara and I had married in the last year of World War II. While I was still majoring in economics at Yale, we talked a lot about doing something different with our lives; and we didn't put any limit on our imagination either.

Once after reading Louis Bromfield's book *The Farm*, we seriously considered going into farming. We were attracted by the idea of being self-sufficient, as well as the basic values Bromfield described as being part of farm life. There were Grant Wood visions of golden wheat fields under blue Midwestern skies and bringing up a family in the farm belt.

Then we started looking more deeply into the economics of life on the farm. Not just what it might take to operate a successful farm, but how much was needed for an initial investment in land, stock and farm equipment. It was more than we could afford: we didn't have the money; we didn't know where to raise it. One thing for certain, it wasn't the sort of business proposition to take up with our families.

My father, Prescott Bush, Sr., was a successful businessman, a partner in the investment banking firm of Brown Brothers, Harriman and Company. He had made money and our family lived comfortably but not ostentatiously. Dad believed in the old Ben Franklin copybook maxims when it came to earning, saving and spending. In other ways, too, he and my mother embodied the Puritan ethic, in the best sense of the term. Their children – my brothers Pres, John and Buck, my sister Nancy and I – all grew up understanding that life is not an open ended checking account. Whatever we wanted, we'd have to earn. From an early age we knew that if an illness or something really serious occurred, our folks would be there to help, but once we left home, we'd make it on our own in business or whatever we entered in later life.

If I'd really believed there was a solid business prospect to discuss, I wouldn't have hesitated to go to Dad. No matter how we looked at it, though, "George and Barbara Farms" came off as a high-risk, no-yield investment.

But there was another, even better reason why Barbara and I never considered going to our families for seed money. As my father had taught me, breaking away meant just that – living on our own. I'd saved up $3,000 in the Navy. Not much, but enough to get us started independently. We were young, still in our early twenties, and we wanted to make our own way, our own mistakes, and shape our own future.

My father first traveled east to go to school. After finishing college at Yale, he enlisted in the Army field artillery when the United States entered World War I. Sent overseas, he rose to the rank of captain, then returned home to begin a career in business management. His father, Samuel P. Bush, was president of Buckeye Steel Casting in Columbus, but Dad wasn't interested in going to work there. He took a job with the Simmons Hardware Company in St. Louis, my mother's hometown.

Dad was a business administrator whose forte was reorganizing failing companies, turning money losers into profit makers. After several years with the Simmons company, he was hired by the creditors of the Hupp Products Company, a floor-covering firm, to straighten out its financial affairs. When Dad pinpointed the problem – in this case, illegal profit skimming – Mr. Hupp took it personally. This led to the kind of crisis management they don't teach in Business Administration 101: my father had to keep a loaded gun in his desk drawer. The situation was finally resolved when Hupp was convicted of swindling. Hupps' creditors asked Dad to stay on and run the small firm. He did, successfully, and after a series of mergers it became part of the United States Rubber Company.

It wasn't until 1950, two years after I'd left for Texas, that Dad entered his first political race, at age 55, as a candidate for the United States Senate. It didn't surprise me, because I knew what motivated him. He'd made his mark in the business world. Now he felt he had a debt to pay.

Newsweek magazine, in a story covering the 1950 Senate campaign, quoted what it called a "hard-boiled political writer" who was covering Dad's race: "Pres had an old-fashioned idea that the more advantages a man has, the greater his obligation to do public service. He believes it and, damn it, I believe him." Dad had been on vacation in Maine when he developed a cough that he didn't seem to be able to shake. He was finally persuaded to go to Sloan-Kettering's Memorial Hospital in New York for a thorough checkup. The diagnosis was lung cancer. He didn't despair, but the disease spread rapidly.

Mother stayed with us at the United Nations Ambassador's residence in the Waldorf Astoria, spending most of her time at Dad's bedside. He died October 8, 1972. It was a real blow for me, for all his children. We had lost a best friend.

TUCKER CARLSON

TUCKER CARLSON is co-host of *Crossfire,* CNN's popular and lively political debate program. Carlson and co-host Robert Novak provide insight and commentary "from the right," as they square off against co-hosts James Carville and Paul Begala "from the left." The show airs live in front of a studio audience from George Washington University's Jack Morton Auditorium in Washington, D.C. In 2002, *Crossfire* celebrated its twentieth anniversary. Carlson is also a political analyst for CNN based in the network's Washington, D.C., bureau.

Most recently, Carlson was co-host of CNN's *Spin Room* with Bill Press. Since 1997, Carlson has provided analysis for *Inside Politics,* the nation's first program devoted exclusively to politics. In 1998, he joined the media roundtable on CNN's Sunday talk show *Late Edition with Wolf Blitzer.*

Carlson writes the National Affairs column for *New York Magazine* and is a contributing editor for *The Weekly Standard*. Previously he was a contributing editor for *Talk* magazine and a writer for the *Arkansas Democrat-Gazette* in Little Rock. Carlson's writing has also appeared in *The Wall Street Journal*, *George*, *The New Republic, Forbes FYI, Slate* and *The Washington Post*.

Carlson earned his bachelor's degree from Trinity College in Connecticut.

I became a journalist for the most medieval of reasons: my father was. By the time I was a child, in the 1970s, he'd become a television reporter and anchor, but in the years before he'd worked out of every possible sort of newsroom. He'd been a wire service reporter, a newspaperman, a magazine writer and combinations of all three. He was a natural journalist and a happy one. He never pushed me to do what he did; I'm not sure he even suggested it. But after growing up with him, I never seriously considered anything else.

By some measures my dad always had conventional jobs. He went to work in the morning, came home at night and collected a paycheck. Yet I always had the feeling that there was something not-quite-mainstream about what he did for a living. It was like he belonged to a secret organization with a slightly different set of rules. He never came out and declared that journalists were exempt from the usual bourgeois regulations, but that was definitely the sense. Watching him, I got the impression that reporters weren't part of the straight world.

For one thing, reporters got to go wherever they wanted. They were allowed to visit war zones, wander into strangers' houses to ask questions, cross the yellow police tape at crime scenes. (My dad let us see this last privilege firsthand one Saturday afternoon, when he led my brother and me past a knot of detectives to get a closer look at a murder victim lying on the sidewalk.) As far as my father was concerned, interesting experiences weren't a perk of journalism, they were the point of it. Journalism was the chance to experience the world, to see things other people didn't. Journalism was adventure. My dad, who had joined the service at 17 after getting bounced out of high school, was strongly pro-adventure.

He was a master at describing what he'd seen. At dinner, or on long drives through Maine in the summertime, we listened for hours – literally hours, without fidgeting – as he recounted news events he'd covered. He'd worked the night beat for years, so naturally mayhem figured prominently in his stories: The betrayed housewife who cut off her husband's nose with a straight razor. The rapist who was knocked off an apartment building fire escape by his victim and was neatly bisected by a stockade fence. The Zodiac killer. The Zebra murders. The Patty Hearst kidnapping. The Watts riots. Warehouse fires, protest marches, unusually grisly suicides. He rendered each scene in Technicolor. It was better than the movies.

His ability to summon ancient facts was amazing. He could remember the name, age and occupation of virtually everybody he'd ever interviewed. He specialized in small but distinctive details. "The only witness was a cab driver," he'd say, "a middle-aged Norwegian guy named Johansson with a waxed crew cut. He'd been a merchant seaman in the Orient in the '50s...."

My father talked like the best writers write. Every sentence advanced the story. He used strong verbs. He hated clichés. Not surprisingly, he was a connoisseur of newspaper headlines. Sometimes he spoke in them. I remember one morning tripping and falling in the kitchen with a box of Cheerios in hand. I hadn't made it off the floor before my father responded, instinctively, with a headline: "Boy Maimed in Bizarre Cereal Mishap." My knees hurt but I laughed anyway. My dad saw the humor in almost everything.

Not everyone got it. Although he was unusually literate – on vacations and weekends, he read a book a day, at least – my dad had a saltiness that other kids' dads didn't. He knew hookers and cops and FBI agents. He smoked unfiltered cigarettes and rode an old flat-head motorcycle to work. When I was in the first grade, he took my brother and me to a Mafia hitman's house for dinner. "He's the guy who killed Bugsy Siegel," my father informed us in the car on the way over.

If it ever occurred to him that it might be risky to hang around with violent people, he never mentioned it. My dad was the least afraid person I've ever known. He didn't swagger or boast about his toughness. He just seemed completely unintimidated by life. It was impossible to imagine him cowering before authority. And he was physically brave. Years later, I had the perverse pleasure of sitting across the aisle from him on an airplane that we both knew was in the process of going down. As the plane fell sideways toward earth and a crash landing, my father reached over, squeezed my hand and smiled. "If we make it out of this, let's get a pizza and a beer," he said. When it was over, we did.

But my father was at his most courageous in conversation. He said precisely what he thought, regardless of the pressure not to. He could do this because he was a journalist. Journalists were allowed to say what they believed to be true, no matter how inconvenient or disruptive. If it's accurate, you get to report it. Those were the rules, at least according to my dad. It took me years to appreciate what a rare blessing this is. Most people aren't encouraged to be perfectly honest at work; some get fired for it. Journalists have that privilege guaranteed in their job descriptions. Even as a child, this struck me as a thrilling idea.

Of course, my father rarely made any of this explicit. He distrusted airy abstractions, and as much as he loved to talk, he hated lecturing. He never referred to the "craft" of reporting or the "sacred trust" between journalists and the public. I think he would have felt foolish. I know he would have eaten dirt before he used the phrase "journalistic ethics," except possibly in an ironic way. Still, my dad considered journalism an honorable career, and said so.

Most of all, he enjoyed tormenting bullies. He took seriously the idea that a free press is society's strongest bulwark against the abuse of power. His definition of abuse of power was broad. His favorite stories were the ones that allowed him to give the finger to some illegitimate authority or other. The one I remember best was a piece he did about the mistreatment of abandoned pets at an animal shelter.

He was working at the ABC station in Los Angeles at the time. Looking back, I can't imagine that his news director considered a pet story very newsworthy. My dad didn't care. He loved animals. (Thirty years after two of his dogs died, he still kept pictures of them in his wallet.) The thought that dogs and cats were being abused by cretins at the pound infuriated him. And, as it turned out, not just him. Viewer response to his story was so strong that within days the director of the shelter was fired. I think it was one of my father's happiest days in journalism.

My dad always said the same thing when he admired somebody:

"He's an interesting guy." It was shorthand. To my father, "interesting" implied a whole range of positive qualities: wisdom, experience, accomplishment, charm. To be interesting meant that you hadn't just existed. You'd done something worthwhile with your life.

My father was an interesting man. I decided at a young age that I wanted to be like him.

PRESIDENT JIMMY CARTER

JAMES EARL CARTER, JR., 39th president of the United States, was born October 1, 1924, in the small farming town of Plains, Georgia, and grew up in the nearby community of Archery.

He was educated in the Plains public schools, attended Georgia Southwestern College and the Georgia Institute of Technology, and received a Bachelor of Science degree from the U.S. Naval Academy in 1946. In the Navy he became a submariner, serving in both the Atlantic and Pacific fleets and rising to the rank of lieutenant.

In 1962 he won election to the Georgia Senate. He lost his first gubernatorial campaign in 1966 but won the next election, becoming Georgia's 76th governor on January 12, 1971. He was the Democratic National Committee campaign chairman for the 1974 congressional and gubernatorial elections.

On December 12, 1974, he announced his candidacy for President of the United States. He won his party's nomination on the first ballot at the 1976 Democratic National Convention and was elected President on November 2, 1976.

Jimmy Carter served as President from January 20, 1977, to January 20, 1981. Significant foreign policy accomplishments of his administration included the Panama Canal treaties, the Camp David Accords, the treaty of peace between Egypt and Israel, the SALT II treaty with the Soviet Union, and the establishment of U.S. diplomatic relations with the People's Republic of China. He championed human rights throughout the world. On the domestic side, the administration's achievements included a comprehensive energy program conducted by a new Department of Energy; deregulation in energy, transportation, communications, and finance; major educational programs under a new Department of Education; and major environmental protection legislation, including the Alaska National Interest Lands Conservation Act.

On December 10, 2002, the Norwegian Nobel Committee awarded the Nobel Peace Prize to Carter "for his decades of untiring effort to find peaceful solutions to international conflicts, to advance democracy and human rights, and to promote economic and social development." Carter is the author of 17 books.

On July 7, 1946, he married the former Rosalynn Smith. They have four children, three boys and one girl.

Because I worked with him and observed his daily activities, my father, James Earl Carter, was the center of my life and the focus of my admiration when I was a child. He was a serious and sometimes stern businessman, but often lively and full of fun with friends and with the men and women who lived on our farm. When I joined him on his routes to sell milk, syrup and other products, I could see how easily he traded with the merchants and filling station owners who were his customers, but without wasting time at each stop. In addition to taking care of business, he was deeply involved in church work, the county school system and other community affairs. Also, he was fascinated with sports and the outdoors, and loved to have a good time when his work was done and financial settlements were complete.

Daddy was a relatively small man, about an inch taller than Mama, but stockily built and very strong for his size. He had light-reddish hair – thinning, perhaps, because he was never outdoors without a hat. Despite this, his face was always sunburned, and his body looked surprisingly white whenever he took off his shirt to go swimming. He was one of the best divers at Magnolia Springs and McMath's Millpond, and an outstanding tennis player. Some of the men would drive out on Sunday afternoons, and unless there was a big group, they usually played singles, with the player who first lost a set dropping out if others were waiting. The winner stayed on the court as long as he wished. Usually that was Daddy.

He was impatient for me to grow up, and began giving me tennis lessons as soon as I was old enough to hold a racquet. Although I eventually became the top player in high school, I could never beat him – and he certainly never gave me a point.

Daddy wore thick eyeglasses, and I never saw him outdoors without that hat – a gray felt fedora during the cold months and a straw Panama hat of the same basic design when the weather was warm. Unfortunately, another constant feature of his appearance was a cigarette in his mouth or hand. With the approval of the government, tobacco companies had distributed free smokes to him and other soldiers during World War I, and he became addicted to the strongest brands, usually smoking at least two packages of Home Runs every day. To save money during the Depression years, he bought gallon cans of tightly packed shredded tobacco, cigarette paper in large packages, and a small machine that my sister Gloria and I used to keep him supplied with home-rolled cigarettes. There were no health warnings in those days, so we didn't know about the almost inevitable cancer that would cause premature death.

My father's independent nature rebelled against an addiction that controlled him, though, and this brought about one of my most memorable conversations with him. One day, about the time I became a teen-ager, I was shocked when Daddy told me to come into the bathroom and shut the door. After desperately trying to remember all my recent activities that might have displeased him, I finally decided that he was going to tell me about the sexual habits of birds and bees.

Instead, he said, using a rare and solemn form of address, "Jimmy, I need to talk to you about something important."

"Yes, sir, Daddy."

I was relieved when he said, "I don't want you to smoke a cigarette until you are 21 years old."

"No, sir, Daddy, I won't."

He then made an unnecessary commitment. "When the time comes, I'll buy you a gold watch."

I kept my promise and so did he. I was a midshipman at the Naval Academy when I reached legal maturity, and I went to the store in Bancroft Hall and bought a package of cigarettes. I took one puff, didn't like it, and never smoked another. Unfortunately, my mother and my three siblings took up Daddy's habit, and all died of cancer.

Some of my best days were when I would go to the professional baseball games in Americus with Mama and Daddy. We sat with my Uncle Buddy on the front row along the first-base line, in chairs reserved for him and the other officials of the Georgia-Florida baseball league. It was Class D ball, an integral part of the immense web of farm systems that existed in those days to feed superior players step by step into the Major Leagues. There were always a few big league players who began their careers in Americus, Cordele or Albany or on one of the other nearby teams. My parents and Uncle Buddy knew every one of them, almost as well as they knew the citizens of Plains.

In addition to learning about working duties on the farm, I was also expected to know about the woods and swamps, and Daddy would teach and quiz me about basic survival techniques.

Once when I was fishing with a friend, Rembert, on Choctahatchee Creek, we found an enormous alligator snapping turtle, the biggest we had ever seen, pinned down by a tree that had fallen on it. It had begun drizzling rain, and it was time to take our poles and leave the creek, so we took all our fishing lines, doubled them up, and suspended the monster from a limb to carry it between us and show it to our parents. It was almost sundown when we started walking out of the swamp. This time I had forgotten my compass, and as dark approached we realized we were lost. I began to get nervous, but a half-hour later we were delighted to see some human tracks – until we realized that they were our own. I remembered how Daddy had told me that it was a natural human inclination to walk around in a circle unless we focused on specific landmarks.

About this time, the weather cleared well enough for us to see the sky, so we abandoned the turtle and begun trotting westward, in a straight line toward Venus, which was then an evening star. We hurried forward, often forcing ourselves through clinging briars and holding up our arms to prevent the low tree limbs from striking us in our faces. After an hour or so, we reached a road, and I knew enough to follow it to the house of a black family – a long way from where I had expected to come out. I was both relieved and concerned to learn that Daddy had already been there, telling the family to be on the lookout for us. We were too exhausted to walk any farther, so the man hitched up his wagon and we began the journey of about eight miles to our home.

I feared confronting my father, knowing the anguish we had caused him and Mama, and how annoyed he would be because I had violated all the woodsman's rules he had taught me. We soon met his pickup and began the long drive back home. Daddy didn't speak to me until we drove up to our house and stood together in the yard. He looked at me for a few minutes and then said, "I thought you knew better than to get lost in the woods."

I began to cry, and he reached out for me. Just being there enfolded in my father's arms was one of the most unforgettable moments of my life.

JAMES CARVILLE

JAMES CARVILLE is a political consultant *extraordinaire*.

He led campaign victories for governors (Robert Casey in Pennsylvania and Zell Miller in Georgia), Senators (Frank Lautenberg in New Jersey and Harris Wofford in Pennsylvania) and – his most stunning – for President William Jefferson Clinton in his victory over incumbent George H.W. Bush in 1992.

Carville was honored as Campaign Manager of the Year by the American Association of Political Consultants and was also the *de facto* star, along with George Stephanopoulos, of the feature-length Academy Award nominated documentary *The War Room.*

Carville currently focuses on foreign consulting. His clients have included presidents and prime ministers from Europe, Brazil and the Caribbean, and in 1999 he led Ehud Barak to victory in his campaign to become prime minister of Israel.

James Carville is also an author, speaker, restaurateur and talk show host. With his wife Mary Matalin, who is currently assistant to President Bush and counselor to Vice-President Cheney, Carville co-wrote *All's Fair: Love, War, and Running for President*, which spent eight weeks on *The New York Times* bestseller list. Carville's next books (*We're Right, They're Wrong: A Handbook for Spirited Progressives; And the Horse He Rode In On: The People vs. Kenneth Starr*; and *Stickin'*) earned long-running places on that prestigious list as well. *Suck Up, Buck Up...and Come Back When You Foul Up*, Carville's latest literary effort, co-written with Paul Begala, details strategies for fighting and winning in business, politics and life. Begala and Carville can also be seen co-hosting CNN'S *Crossfire*.

James Carville resides in Virginia with his wife and two daughters.

I guess my earliest recollection and most lasting memory of my father was that he was a very gentle man. He worked a lot and he worked hard. He ran a general store that was attached to the post office in Carville, Louisiana, where he was the postmaster, like his father and his father before that. When he died in 1978, it was the first time a Carville did not hold the post since the turn of the 20th century.

He opened the store at 7:00 a.m. and closed it at 6:00 p.m., six days a week, and as soon as he came home to his kids (I have seven siblings and we were always a growing family, since I was the oldest), we'd make him come out and throw baseballs with us. Then he'd go back in and everyone would eat off his plate and jump all over him. One of the things we all talk about now is how when he came home, he loved to fix a deli plate that included some shrimp, some salami, maybe a little cheese. At night in the South when I grew up, you'd either eat leftovers or something cool. So as soon as he would come home, we'd be all over him. It would take him four plates before he got anything to eat. I think about that when I come home, as an older parent, and my own children are always jumping on me.

He just wasn't a guy that complained very much. His gentleness had such a great influence on the way I am around my kids. I've never dreamed of spanking my children or anything like that. Discipline was not his thing. Disappointment was the way he kept things in check. He was just the kind of guy you didn't want to disappoint.

My father was always kind of fascinated by politics. He always discussed what was going on. He was not nearly as aggressive as I am – that came from my mother. But he was informed from reading the papers (the *Baton Rouge Advocate* in the morning and the *Picayune* from New Orleans in the afternoon) from front to back. He'd often talk about events of the day and was definitely up on things.

His real influence on me came after I got married and had kids of my own, because I never knew him as a single guy.

He was a very well liked man. I don't think he was ever feared nor set out to be so. He was almost loved by his community. He grew up and never left the same zip code, other than to go in the Army. When he went to college, he traveled only 25 or 30 miles north, because the LSU campus was on the same side of town that we were.

Sports were important to us as a family. Dad was a boxer during the 1930s at LSU. He was a good athlete. I played Little League baseball in Baton Rouge, and it took 45 minutes to get to the game back then. But he never missed one Little League game, and he or my mother drove me into practice every day. It was the same thing in football, track and basketball. The only time he could not make it was once or twice when we were on the road in high school, because the games were so far away. Some took four hours to reach.

It was a big thing of his that no child, and he had eight kids, was going to look up off of a playing field and not see his or her parents there. That was a huge, huge thing. When on a few occasions he couldn't make a game, he was very distraught.

The unique thing about him (and nowadays it is hard to believe that it was special, but it was unique at the time) is that he allowed no pejoratives about anyone or anything in his house. We were not allowed to use the "n" word, which you can imagine was every other word with some in the Deep South of the 1950s. There was an Italian community nearby and someone used the "d" word, and he just went berserk.

He did not like people talking ugly about one another. If, in fact, they are right that it's "The Golden Rule" and then everything else, then he's in pretty good shape. Even though he was not a man who wanted great change in his world, he was certainly unusual in his beliefs for his times. Even now when I go home to Baton Rouge, racist things come out of people's mouths. If you called black people "colored" back then, you were a raving liberal. It was a real dividing line.

My father grew up in a place that was 85 percent black, and the dominant business was the U.S. Public Health Service Hospital where everybody worked and treated Hanson's Disease or leprosy. It meant that people from all over the world came to Carville. I've had people go to Carville to see where I came from, and they were stunned at how rural it is. But there was integration in the workplace, and even though nowhere was a good place to be a black in the South in the '50s, Carville was not a bad place, mainly because the government was hiring everyone and they took anti-discrimination into account when making policy.

Back in 1994, on the one-hundredth anniversary of the hospital, I went back and met with many folks, including doctors, patients and others, and I was surprised and really gratified at how well they spoke of my father. They told how when they came in the store they were always treated with respect, and how the Post Office would try to do everything they could to help. My father was just a very gentle guy. I don't know whether it was a birth order thing or what. He was something more than just a good man – that I'm positive of.

CALVIN "CAL" DARDEN

CAL DARDEN is Senior Vice President of U.S. Operations for UPS. He manages 320,000 employees and $24 billion in revenues. His operational responsibilities include ensuring that UPS meets it commitments for the pick-up and delivery of 12.4 million packages every day.

A native of Buffalo, New York, Darden attended Canisius College and received a Bachelor of Science degree in business management in 1972. He joined UPS in 1971 as a part-time package handler and was promoted to positions of increasing responsibility.

Darden is a member of the UPS Management Committee, which directs the day-to-day management of the company. He has also served as a member of the UPS Board of Directors since 2001. In keeping with his own long-standing commitment to the community, Darden is on the Board of Directors of the National Urban League. He belongs to the 100 Black Men of North Metro Atlanta, is involved with the United Way, and serves as a deacon at his church. He is also on the Board of Directors for Target Corporation and Coca-Cola Enterprises.

Darden was ranked eighth on *Fortune's* listing of the 50 Most Powerful Black Executives in America before his retirement in 2005.

He is married and has three children.

My father was born and raised in Tuscaloosa, Alabama, and went into the service when he was 19 or 20 years old. He served three years and then wound up settling in Buffalo, New York, where I was born and raised. He worked for 25 years as a core maker with American Standard in Tonawanda, New York, where they made bathtubs and toilets.

I was always very impressed by my father, who unfortunately passed away in 1985 from lung cancer. He provided for seven children, and I am still mystified how he did it. He was making only $150-200 a week, which maybe back then was a lot of money, but we never wanted for food or clothes nor had the electricity turned off. My mother was the homemaker, so she raised us. To keep us out of trouble, Dad always kept us busy. The four boys stayed mostly with him. To supplement his income, my father would do remodeling – installing ceilings or paneling, and other home improvements – and we learned how to do all of that. Then in the summer we would go fishing, and in the winter we would go hunting. Dad was very religious, so he took us to church whether we wanted to go or not. Now my children go to church because it flowed right on through the family. Dad instilled in us that religious values are very, very important because we need God's leadership to direct us where we need to go.

My father did not have a formal education, but he always said to us, "I want you to go to school to get a good education. I want you to study hard because I will not be able to afford to send you to school. I need you and your brothers and sisters to win scholarships." And that is exactly what I did. I won a four-year academic scholarship to Canisius College in Buffalo. All of my siblings also earned scholarships.

One of the things I love about working for UPS is that it has been almost a seamless transition from my personal upbringing. The family and ethical values that my father taught me were so evident at UPS. I learned that very quickly, and it has kept me around for 32 years.

There are so many lessons my father tried to teach me as a child that I did not fully understand. Things he would not allow me to do or things he said that I did not appreciate at the time. I understand them clearly now.

I had to go to bed at 8:30 every night. People always ask me why I get up so early, but it is because my father instilled that "early to bed, early to rise" mentality from day one. I understand now that it was his way of making sure we were not up to no good, but it took a while. When you are a kid and your parents tell you "Don't go there," or "Don't do that," sometimes it does not register. Of course, once you have your own children, you understand what they were telling you.

I was taught that the father was head of the household. It was his responsibility to think not only about the day-to-day, but also about what was coming down the road in order to prepare the family. It was the father's job to hold the house together, and if something bad happened, it was his fault. I still believe that to be correct. If there are decisions to be made, the father needs to make the right ones for the family. I have instilled this belief in my children.

He vividly explained the difference between a dad and a father. Anybody can father a child, but it takes a dad to raise a child. That means you never walk away from your children. It is necessary to make sure, from the age of zero all the way to adulthood, that you are doing what is necessary to get this little guy or girl what is needed. That always rang very true with me.

Dad also taught us to help others. Not only your brothers and sisters, but others who are less fortunate. He always said that no matter what state or condition you were in, no matter how bad you felt, there was always someone who was worse off. You need to lend a helping hand to that person. It did not have to be monetary, because there were other ways you could help, so he always taught us to do that.

My father used to take us to "Sunrise Court," which convenes at 6:00 a.m. on Sunday in Buffalo. He sat us on the back row of the courtroom while they brought out all the drug addicts and prostitutes that had been arrested the night before. He told us, "If you do not get a good education, this is where you will end up." It was a "scared straight" thing, and I will always remember it. It was an eye-opening experience to see those folks being dragged in with handcuffs in front of the judge. It really hammered home the feeling and the urge to stay on the straight and narrow path.

My father taught us the moral values of life. He talked about integrity, about not getting in trouble with the law. He taught us not to get into drugs and not to hang out on the street corners. He said, "If you ever go to jail, you will stay there, because I will never come bail you out – you can bet on that."

My father was six feet five inches tall and weighed 280 pounds. I think he meant everything he said.

RON DELSENER

Since 1964, **RON DELSENER** has been at the forefront of outdoor popular-music concerts. He began his career in concert promotion by co-producing The Beatles' first outdoor concert performance in New York during the summer of 1964 at the outdoor Forest Hills Stadium in Queens, New York. Prior to this chapter in American music history, outdoor pop-music concerts were rare, except for a handful of concerts held at the Hollywood Bowl and the Carter Barron Amphitheater in Washington, D.C.

Since his incredible beginning and emergence as one of the great promoters in American pop culture history, Delsener has produced some of the most famous acts in the world in some of the largest arenas (both indoor and out) on the planet. These include Billy Joel, The Who, Louis Armstrong, Miles Davis, Benny Goodman, Otis Redding, Bobby Darin, Muddy Waters, Neil Diamond, Stevie Wonder, Sly & the Family Stone, Led Zeppelin, The Grateful Dead and many others. For years he produced $1 admission and then free concerts in New York's Central Park, first at the Sheep Meadow and later on the Great Lawn. The series became the hallmark by which most other outdoor concert series are judged.

Delsener has also acted as producer for more than a dozen Broadway shows, including "Bette Midler at the Palace," "Bette Midler:

Clams on the Half Shell," "Gilda Live from New York," and Lily Tomlin in "Appearing Nightly." His most recent off-Broadway successes were the highly-acclaimed "Sandra Bernhard – I'm Still Here...Damn It" and "The Exonerated."

Delsener has produced a large number of benefit concerts for a variety of charitable organizations, including the No-Nukes Concert, Tribute to Nelson Mandela at Yankee Stadium and Eric Clapton's Crossroads Rehabilitation Center in Antigua.

He and his wife, Ellin, have one daughter, Samantha, one grandson and one granddaughter. They reside in East Hampton, New York.

I always thought my father was born in Hudson Falls, New York, because that is where the family lived, but he was actually born in San Benedetto del Tronto in Italy. It is a large fishing village and beach resort on the Adriatic Sea in the province of Marquis, south of Ancona. My grandfather, Eugenio Delzampo, who came over when he was about 15, started out with an apple stand, gained some success and expanded. He took over a store where he sold fruit, ice cream and groceries. But he went back to Italy and – as the story was told to me by my aunt Minnie – married the prettiest girl in town. She became my grandmother.

My grandparents took a boat back to America after taking a train all the way across Italy. They came here and had two sons and two daughters. When my grandmother became pregnant with my father, they decided they wanted him to be born in Italy, so they went back and he was born in San Benedetto. He was named Ercole, which means Hercules. My father moved with his family to the Bronx and finally settled in Astoria, Queens, where my grandfather opened a newsstand and soda fountain. When he was older, my father opened a driving school, and that's where he met my mother. She was Jewish and came from a family of 11. At the time, it was unheard of for people of two different religious backgrounds, Catholic and Jewish, to date, so my uncles used to chaperone them anywhere they went. But their love was strong and they eventually got married and moved into a cockroach-infested apartment in Astoria.

He worked trimming windows in those early years. If it was Thanksgiving, he would decorate storekeepers' windows with cardboard turkeys. If it was Christmas, it was Santa Claus. They did a really great job – like Barney's does today. They would work with everything from *papier-mache´* to silk. Eventually he saved a little money and moved us to Flushing, Queens, in a little house they bought for $2,500.

This was when America was really America. It was during World War II and there were blackouts, and we had shades on our windows and when the air raid sirens would sound you would pull them down to shut out the light. Then my dad would go play poker in the basement. I remember sitting on his lap while he smoked his cigar, fiddled with his chips and played cards with his friends.

He began selling cosmetics and used to take me to the various dime stores and chain stores like Lamston's and Kresge's. F.W. Woolworth was the big one. I would sit in the car and wait for my father while he called on the buyers to sell to them. Sometimes we would go into the stores and sit down and have baked macaroni or a chocolate ice cream soda or a banana split. He would meet with the manager or the girls behind the counter. He would also trim windows for them sometimes. Those are the first memories I have of him, on his sales rounds.

My room at our house was in a converted attic and the heat was overwhelming. So when air conditioners came out, he gave one to me, the prince of the family. They stuck it in with me, and I remember many nights when they would drag their mattresses up to my room and everyone would sleep on the floor. But, of course, I – the prince – never got out of bed. I should have let my mother have the bed. What a schmuck I was. She should have said get out, but she and my father loved me so much they never did.

He used to take me to the Jamaica racetrack (which is now Aqueduct) to watch the great jockeys of the day ride horses. My father was a big horseplayer, along with his friends. They would push me under their coats and sneak me in. They would teach me how to read the horse form and how to play the horses. If I would lose, I would come home and cry and my mother would tell me to never gamble. In a roundabout way he showed me the ills, and to this day I am not a gambler.

We would go to the Columbia University football games when they had a great team. I was there with him in 1947 when they beat a previously undefeated Army team. We stood around for an hour afterwards in a wonderful kind of shock. We used to go to all the basketball games at Madison Square Garden, the old Garden at 50th Street. He would give the guy at the box office some cosmetics to make sure we got good seats.

My father rarely used any kind of profanity, and if he ever did it was usually an Italian curse word. It was the only Italian he knew. If I said anything bad, I would get my mouth washed out by this red soap called Roseech. It was a kosher soap that was disgusting tasting.

He taught me to dress nicely. I was always having kids laugh at me or throw spitballs at the movies when I would take a date, because I would wear a jacket and long pants, not shorts, and a tie when I was 12 years old. I was always a little more serious, and it carried on through life. When those guys who made fun of me were hanging around the local tavern in Bayside, I did not even drink or smoke. They would be getting wasted. Those guys are probably all dead now. They all had mediocre jobs. But my father taught me not to wait for my ship to come in; he told me to row out and meet it. I will never forget that slogan.

I would take jobs after school, even when I was seven years old. I had a little red wagon and my father would give me some of his products to sell. I would bring shaving cream and cosmetics door to door in the neighborhood with my wagon. I sold Christmas decorations right after the war in 1945, '46 and '47. I would not care if you were Jewish; I would knock on all the doors because I was from a mixed marriage. There was no such thing as "religious" in my house. We just deeply believed in everybody being wonderful.

He always played catch with me in the street, taught me sportsmanship and told me not to be a sore loser, shake hands with everybody and look them in the eye.

He taught me how to drive.

He taught me how to Simonize the car.

He taught me how to barbecue.

I lived with my parents until I got married at 29 and, in many ways, it was the key to my success. If I had not, if they did not let me stay to do laundry and eat meals with them, I would never have found my true calling with a job that suited me best.

My first real job was in advertising, but I used to promote shows for City of Hope, a cancer hospital. I learned how to promote by doing shows for the Catholic schools, among others, in the area. I had a lot of balls. I would go to Broadway and see Dick Van Dyke and go backstage and hustle him into performing for one of my shows. I would call them the "Show of Stars." It got in my blood. I caught the bug.

I went to work for a couple of guys who were doing concerts at the Forest Hills Tennis Stadium after I begged them for a job. They hired me for $75 a week because the guy that was doing the job before me was making $200 and they could save a little money. The only reason *I* could afford to work there was because I lived at home with my parents.

In 1964 at Forest Hills we had the Beatles' first outdoor show, we produced Bob Dylan opening for Joan Baez, and Barbara Streisand and Woody Allen each performed separately. I was determined to become a success. I did have a great amount of accomplishment, but my family life may have suffered as a result.

I have one daughter who is 34 and she has two children, my grandchildren. I was not as good a father with her as my father was with me. It was a different era. He would always get us together to do things like playing miniature golf. That was a big thing. We would go over to friends' homes. It may have been people he did business with, but they were always nice. My parents took us wherever they went. They took us to the theater to see *South Pacific* and *Oklahoma.* On special occasions, like birthdays and their anniversary, we would go out to restaurants. They instilled a sense of family togetherness. My father took me to World Series games at Yankee Stadium, to fights at the Garden – all the sporting events. He did so much more than I did.

With my daughter, I was never home. I am getting a chance to make amends through my grandchildren, whom I see at least two or three times a week, but I never thought of family first as a young father. I thought of making money first, and therefore the act, the performer, was more important than my family. My priority was to kiss the act's ass, do whatever you had to do. There were so many nights when I came home late, went in my daughter's room and the only contact I would have was giving her a kiss goodnight while she was asleep. I did not do the things my father did with me with my own daughter. My wife sacrificed and brought my daughter up great, but I definitely missed doing the things that I see my daughter doing now with her own children.

The lesson I have learned is this: I am going to take this guilt to the grave. Do not overlook your family. Your family comes first. Forget about the business people, because they are not going to come to your aid if you are in trouble. If you did not have something they wanted, they would not bother with you. I was nicer to strangers on my way up than I was to my parents. I belittled them and told them they could not relate to the difficulty of my business. I would go through a tough time at work and take it out on my own family. I regret it and wish I could undo it.

Just remember: the only people who will come help you in the middle of the night when your car breaks down on the expressway are your family. They will come pick you up. They will make you a meal. There is no one like your parents. Nobody is like family.

This is what I have learned.

RICHARD "BO" DIETL

BO DIETL is an internationally recognized private investigator and security consultant with more than 25 years of investigative and security experience. He is one of the most highly decorated detectives in the history of the New York City Police Department. As a detective with the NYPD, Dietl investigated numerous homicides and other serious felonies. During his career he was responsible for more than 1,500 felony arrests, with a remarkable 95 percent conviction rate.

Dietl ran for the U.S. Congress in 1986. Despite endorsements from then-President Ronald Reagan, Vice President George Bush and Senator Alfonse D'Amato, as well as the *New York Times* and the *New York Post,* his election bid was unsuccessful.

Dietl has been a guest lecturer on criminal justice topics at Syracuse University and Central Connecticut State University. He is the author of *One Tough Cop: The Bo Dietl Story* and was also the executive producer of *One Tough Cop: The Bo Dietl Story,* a motion picture released in the fall of 1998.

As a father, Bo has always been deeply concerned about children's issues, specifically protection and safety. He has been the driving force behind computer software products that allow parents to monitor their children's activities on the internet, which, for all of its benefits, also provides predators unfettered access to our homes and our children. Bo and his wife and children live in New York City.

I really had a remarkable relationship with my father.

He taught us never to take anything from anyone without working for it. Whenever my uncles would come over, they would try to give us a quarter, but we could never accept it. I started working when I was seven years old delivering newspapers with my nine-year-old brother. We would wake up in the morning and get 76 papers. I remember it distinctly because there was one apartment house that we delivered to. I used to do all that before I went to school in the morning, while it was still dark out.

When I got a little older, maybe 11, my father took me to the restaurant where he worked, and I got on as a busboy. At 17 I graduated from high school and became a construction worker, where I worked on the World Trade Center. I always worked because my father taught me that if you want something, you work for it.

It was a different time when I grew up. My father was a person who was extremely strict. My mother was born in Sicily and he was born in Germany. He worked six days a week as a chef; in fact, he worked in the food business all his life. I came from an honest upbringing. I would not call us poor but we were not rich. We lived in a small home and my mother worked all the time. So growing up I learned how to iron shirts, clean our home, and prepare the dinner. I was in charge of making the potatoes every night. Yes, every goddamn night we had potatoes – I thought potatoes were the thing! But when my father got home at 5:00 p.m., if I had talked back to my mother or said a cross word to her, my father would – with one motion – open the door, take off his belt and imprint his initials, FD, on my ass from his buckle. Our bathtub had legs on it, and I used to crawl under a six-inch space to get away from that belt. I mean, I love my father, whom I got to know only after I became a man, but he took no crap.

I was brought up in Ozone Park, Queens, with some pretty rough guys. They belonged to organized crime with John Gotti. We all used to hang around on the corner. Now, these guys did some very bad, very illegal things. Up until the time I was 16 years old, I had to be home at 9:00 p.m. If I got home one minute after 9:00, the belt would come off again. You have to understand, this was a time – the early 1960s – when every kid in Ozone Park was shooting heroin. Drugs were more prevalent than ever before. In my neighborhood every kid was trying junk. I am talking about me holding the fuckin' strap while my buddies are doing the syringe in the arm. I am 12 years old and holding some big Mafia wiseguy's kid's arm while they shot heroin! But their fathers loved me because I would walk around with short sleeves – which meant I was not doing it – and I was the National Physical Fitness champion at school. My father was just looking out for me by being strict.

As we got older, in our teenage years, those same guys were doing a lot of car hijackings at Kennedy Airport and such. I was so frightened of my father, and what he would do to me if I was ever caught, that I never got involved. In my house, if you got in trouble you were never innocent, whether you were right, wrong or indifferent. In my house, the police were always right.

My father was not a very warm person. He never kissed me, never did know how to hug me. But I have made sure to hug and kiss all four of my kids. I never hit my children. I laugh when people tell me, "You are the product of an abusive father." That's B.S. I was a tough cop, a tough detective and proved it by being one of the original undercover decoys out there, exposed over 500 times. In many ways my toughness came from him and it served me well. But it does not mean I wanted to treat my kids the same way. My kids get whatever they want; I spoil them rotten. My behavior is my response to how my father was with me. In a roundabout way, it was a lesson that I learned about how to be a parent.

I realize that fear and what my father did to me were the reasons I didn't go the other way into crime, as opposed to law enforcement. If not for him, I would have definitely become a wiseguy or a criminal. And the work ethic he instilled in me speaks for itself. I went from being a cop to detective to one of the most famous guys ever to come out of the New York Police Department. Now I head up my own investigation and security company and do a number of other entrepreneurial things. I was known as, and had a reputation of being, a very tough guy. In 1986 I ran for Congress when my father was still alive, and it made him exceptionally proud. He raised me very well.

The honesty that my father instilled in me, the honesty that I have in my personality, prevails over all. If I do not like somebody, I will tell them. I never talk behind people's backs. I think people find it refreshing, and even though I am a little rough around the edges, what you see is what you get.

Just like with my father.

ARTHUR DONOVAN

ART DONOVAN is one of the "gentle giants" of professional football, an archetype of the old pro lineman – feared on the field yet admired everywhere else for his generous and outgoing personality.

Born in the Bronx, Donovan attended Mt. Saint Michael High School before serving with the Marines in World War II in the Pacific. Afterwards he attended Boston College and graduated in 1950 with a Bachelor of Arts degree. Donovan joined the Baltimore Colts of the NFL in 1950. For the next 12 years, he was an outstanding defensive tackle, chosen to play in five Pro Bowl Games and starring on two World Championship teams (1958 and 1959).

The Colts retired his jersey, number 70, when he retired from professional football in 1960. In 1968, he was paid the greatest tribute by being inducted into the Pro Football Hall of Fame.

His father, Arthur Donovan, Sr., was a famous boxing referee who worked more championship fights than anyone else, including most of Joe Louis's fights.

His grandfather, Mike O'Donovan, born September 27, 1847, was a boxer known as "Professor Mike." He fought from 1866-1891, including two unsuccessful tries for the middleweight championship. He also lost to legends John L. Sullivan and Jack "Nonpareil" Dempsey. He died March 24, 1918. "Professor Mike" was inducted into the

Bronx Hall of Fame in June 1998 in the pioneer category, joining his son Arthur and making them the first father-son to be so honored.

At present, Art Donovan, Jr., resides in Baltimore and is the owner/manager of the Valley Country Club.

Artie Donovan played professional football in the NFL before salary caps, before supplements and long before intense physical training was commonplace, as it is today. His nickname was "Fatso" and he prided himself on his ability to eat more Spam than anyone could ever serve him. He is a jolly, warm and considerate man. His home was Irish and Roman Catholic; he went to a high school run by the archdiocese and lived the golden rule and learned respect for right and wrong.

"My mother would always pack my father's bag before a big fight. He would call the boxing commission the day of the fight, or they would call him (referees never know until the day of the bout if they will be officiating), and then I would go meet him to bring his stuff. One time, I'll never forget, it was before the Joe Louis versus Lou Nova fight in the Polo Grounds. I got the bag and went to wait where my father told me to meet him at 50th street and Madison Square Garden.

"Well, he had forgotten where he told me to meet him, but he finally comes along and grabs the bag and says, 'See you later tonight,' meaning after the fight, and he streaks off. Well, I was supposed to be going with him and I didn't have a nickel to take the train back home. So I found this police captain and told him my name was Arthur Donovan, and that my father was the fight referee and he was so nervous about tonight's fight that he forgot to bring me with him. This nice cop walks me through the gate and puts me on the train and everything ended real nice. We respected the cops and we respected the law.

"My father was a tough guy," Artie reflects. "One time he got hit by a car outside our house. Broke his leg in three places. He went to the V.A. hospital for a time and walked out of there without a crutch.

That's tough. You shoulda seen the car!"

It's that same brand of toughness that made Artie a gridiron legend at Mt. St. Michaels, a standout performer at Boston College, a United States Marine and a pro football Hall of Famer. But he didn't start out as the tough guy; in fact, he started much more humbly because of his father.

"My father was always working. He was a big shot in New York. I learned to box with him down at the Saturday Morning Boys Club at the New York Athletic Club, where he was the boxing instructor. I used to go down and box with him and then box with the members' sons, and he says, 'You can't win,' so I always threw the fights. I was like a punching bag. But it was good training for taking on guys in football because it taught me quickness. I was very slow – they wouldn't even time me in the 40 yard dash, because they were embarrassed."

One of Arthur Jr.'s greatest gifts is story telling. His tales of everything from the Marines to the NFL, mixed with his good humor and honesty, make him a hit on the talk show and banquet circuit. He learned this skill from his dad. "Naturally, he had a lot of stories about the fights he refereed. So when my uncles and cousins would get together, he'd tell them. My father did all the big fights. In 35 years he did 21 Joe Louis fights, including two with Schmeling, middleweight championships, light heavyweights, you name it and he did it. He used to come to training camp with me for two weeks every year, and everyone from the players to the coaches to the newspaper guys would eat it up. They were great stories."

Both father and son were relatively famous, and from an early age Artie learned to respect the fans and enjoy the notoriety. "I remember walking down the Grand Concourse in the Bronx, when my father was in the prime of refereeing. People kept stopping him to get his autograph and he signed every one and talked to them a little bit and answered their questions. He was very nice, very patient. I thought it was the greatest thing ever to happen."

Arthur Donovan grew up in a different era. It was a time when elderly women could walk the streets of the Bronx without fear, a time when neighbors and neighborhoods were nurturing. And when a guy from the neighborhood came back, no matter how much success he had achieved, he remembered his roots. Artie Donovan still remembers where he came from.

HILARY DUFF

HILARY DUFF has succeeded in the worlds of television, film and music. She has starred in her own television series, the highest rated Disney Channel original movie in history, released a platinum selling album and co-starred with Steve Martin on the silver screen.

All this before her seventeenth birthday.

Hilary started her television career at the age of six performing on television and stage – she even acted with the legendary Sean Connery in the play, *Playing By Heart.* Her big break came when she was chosen to play the lead and title character in the television serial *Lizzie Maguire,* which has since won various awards, including the highly sought after Nickelodeon Kids Choice Award.

Her music career has seen her release Christmas carol compilations, movie soundtracks and pop-chart-topping original work. *Metamorphosis* – her appealing debut solo album of 13 songs – shipped well in excess of gold with 800,000 copies on August 26, 2003, and charted No. 2 on the *Billboard* 200 its first week of release.

Her latest frontier has been film. In her motion picture debut, Hilary co-starred with Frankie Muniz in the action-adventure hit *Agent Cody Banks.* In her next major release, 20th Century Fox's *Cheaper By the Dozen,* she shared the credits with aforementioned perennial box office superstar Steve Martin. She also appeared in Warner Bros.' *A*

Cinderella Story.

Hilary has already sold more than three million albums, spent six weeks in the *Billboard* Top 10 and earned two platinum album awards. She has starred in one No. 1 television series, two hit movies and two more major films. Plus, two television specials honored the big day she turned "Sweet Sixteen."

Duff serves on the board of the Audrey Hepburn Children's Benefit Fund and the Celebrity Council of Kids With a Cause.

She lives with her parents, sister and two dogs in their homes in Houston and Los Angeles.

Even though our family does not live together all the time, we are very close. Since my sister Haley and I decided to be actors and have begun to go back and forth from our home in Texas to California where we work, we have a permanent residence on the West Coast, too. My dad is in Texas because of his work, and he comes to visit us about every three weeks, we go back for the big holidays and we talk on the phone every day. We remain really close.

When we were little, my dad always set a good example for my sister and me to look up to. He used to take us on bike rides, and we would pick up all the trash and cans in the neighborhood to keep it clean so it would be a nice place to live. It makes it a better place for everybody. We would recycle and get money that we would donate to homeless people. He is just a really good man with a giving heart.

My parents have always been involved in charity work and would put on Christmas parties with a purpose when we were younger. Instead of people bringing presents, they would bring diapers and baby food, and my mom and dad would take it to the shelters during Christmas time. Helping through charity has been something that my dad has always practiced, and my sister and I have always been taught to give back. It makes you feel good and does such positive things.

My dad is a very smart man and extremely hard working. But he has a great sense of humor and is totally hilarious. When I had one of my birthday parties in Texas, my first boy-girl party, it was a big deal that boys were coming and we were going to dance. So when we were all dancing, my dad came out the door doing the Chuck Berry guitar boogie dance. Oh my gosh, I wanted to kill him! Doing that dance in front of all my friends. He was thinking he looked really cool. I was so embarrassed! I told him with gritted teeth, "Go inside. NOW!" But now that I'm older that stuff does not bother me, because I know he is just trying to embarrass me. I just think he is really funny.

Every time he comes to town, we get a small lecture from Dad. Like, if Mom tells him that "Hilary gave me attitude today," I get a little talking to, but he is really cool about it. We spend more time with my mom but when we see Dad, he always tells us that we need to help out around the house and pitch in more, to give back and be nicer and thankful.

He and his partners own a chain of convenience stores all over Texas, so he would always get these signs from the stores that teach us a little lesson, like "Feed your own dog," and other cheesy things like that. But he would also give them to us to encourage us with sayings like "Don't be followers," or, "Don't let others influence you," and, "Be your own person."

A lot of times fame can be very hard. When it first started, I thought it was really cool that people wanted my autograph and wanted to take pictures with me. Now it is still very flattering, because I would not be able to do this if it were not for those people out there that come up to me every single day. But there is a time for it and a time not for it. When I am sitting down with my family for dinner, it is hard to be interrupted, or if I am trying to shop after not having a day off for a long time, I just want to be left alone. It sounds kind of bitter to put it that way, but sometimes we cannot even go to the grocery store without running into people with cameras waiting, or sometimes people even knock on our door at home. There was a time when I would ask why this was happening to me, and my dad would be the first person to say, "Hilary, this is your life now. If you don't like it, we can go back to Texas and you can be a regular kid. But you still have to be good to these people even when you have hard days." So I think about that every once in a while and I am very thankful that people come up to me, because if they did not, my life would be very different.

I want to be just as smart as my dad. He is very into his work. I am very driven. When I want something, I really want it, and I am going to try and do everything I can to get it with my work. But my dad is not tolerant at all for being unintelligent, for making little mistakes. It is not that he is not patient, just that he expects a lot, and that's not a bad thing at all.

If there was one thing I could change about him, it would be to make him a slower swimmer so I could beat him racing in the pool. Whenever he comes into town, we always play in the pool and he is a really fast swimmer. Now that I am older I can pretty much beat him, but when I was little he would not cut me any slack. He would never let me win, but if I could make him laugh real hard during the race, I would always beat him.

The newest hobby I have with my dad is driving. I cannot always drive with my mom because she is not as patient as he is. He will be much more calm and tell me "There is a car coming over there," or, "Here comes a stop sign," or, "Yield," or, "Slow down a little." But my mom will say, "Stop, stop, STOP! Ahhhh!" So then we'll argue because I do not want to listen to her when I am driving, because I think I know it all even though I do not. Dad is just a little more mellow, so whenever he is in town, we drive around the entire time.

Nobody in our family is an actor or actress. My and my sister's talent and desire did not really come from either one of our parents. But they have always been such super, supportive parents. Playing sports, like in soccer, my dad was always one of the coaches. When I was in gymnastics, he was always there. Then when Haley wanted to be an actress, and so did I because she was my older sister, and when she wanted to be a singer and so I wanted to be one too, he was so supportive of Haley's and my dreams. The one thing that I think is the greatest thing about my dad is that everything that is very important to my sister and me is very important to him.

ALAN "BOSTON" DVORKIS

ALAN DVORKIS is one of the premier professional gamblers in America today. He is a bookmaker's nightmare because of his incredibly meticulous preparation and because he wins – a lot. He is considered the foremost bettor in the area of NCAA men's basketball. "Boston," as he is known to his friends and foes alike, has a degree in biological behavior from the University of Pennsylvania. He lives five months per year in Las Vegas and the remainder at a beach house in southern Maine. His goal is to become a high school English teacher and to live full time someplace outside of Vegas.

Alan's roots are in a lower middle-class suburb of Boston. When asked where he grew up, he responds "I haven't!" After the laughter subsides, he adds "This the way I am. I can't help it.

"Actually, I started out in Brighton, Massachusetts, and then as the whole world moved to the suburbs, we did too. The name of the town was Framingham – it was about 20 miles outside of Boston. My dad still drives a taxicab in Boston, which has made his life a full circle because that's what he did when I was born. He tried to break out of it when he worked in a lumberyard, but he hit a glass ceiling. He achieved the highest managerial job but got held back without the education. Now he's back driving that cab. It taught me the value of going to school."

Boston was introduced to gambling at a young age and took to it for more than just the adrenaline rush that hooks so many. He saw it as a way of fitting in and a way to spend time with his father.

"I think my dad was a good father. I have no knock at all. He is the major influence in what I have become, because how else are you going to find a race track when you are eight or nine years old?

"The most obvious influence my father had on my life is that he was a gambler. He had a keen interest in harness racing, which is a big New England game that has filtered down to New York and New Jersey. Since I wanted to hang out with my dad, I never minded going along.

"One time we went up to New Hampshire to watch a friend's horse race. I was probably no more than nine years old. The horse won by a nose and it was a real rush. It was like, 'Wow, that's kinda cool!' As I got older, I would always find excuses to try and go to the track with him. I remember a Little League game that I left because my father's own horse was racing and he had to go watch it. I was 11.

"In high school, I always finished my homework really quick so I could sneak off to the track for a few races. It ultimately became a very comfortable and happy place to be. At the age of 13 I was very introverted, and the track was a safe place, the place I'd go to get by. It allowed me to avoid a lot of teen issues. That bullshit doesn't seem important now, but when I was younger I just wanted to play it safe, and the track was how I played it safe. So I owe that to my father, because he took me there and I enjoyed it."

Nowadays Boston is, in many circles, the toast of Vegas. He often places bets of up to $30,000 on games, and to have six figures laid out is commonplace. He wins more than he loses and lives a life commensurate with any successful, fortyish professional. How does his father feel about his chosen career? "He loves my success. He is more proud of me than if I had become a doctor or a lawyer. He is overtly proud. He once told me, 'If you receive respect from your peers, you've accomplished a lot in life,' and he understands that people respect me for my ability and my honesty. That was extremely important to him. He always encouraged doing the right thing. Do the right thing, even against all adversity – that was his motto."

So what does the future hold for Alan "Boston" Dvorkis?

"Right now I live part-time in Vegas and part-time in Maine, but I hope to make it full-time in Maine. Ultimately I want to teach high school English. That's the goal I'm working towards now. To me, that is taking the ultimate gamble, and I think it will really make me a better person. Gambling to me is not about risk, it's about playing it safe, because if I did anything else I'd be uncomfortable. I'm no success story. I'll be successful when I go teach and help those kids to learn."

If his track record is any indication, bet the house on it.

PAT DYE, JR.

PAT DYE, JR. is one of the premier NFL agents and the son of legendary former Auburn University football coach Pat Dye. "Pat's clients are all strong character guys, and that is pretty much a reflection of Pat. There aren't a lot of guys in his line of work that I would trust if I had a kid who needed an agent, but he is one of 'em." Who gives such high praise to Pat Dye, Jr.? None other than the premier NFL coach of the last 25 years, Bill Parcells. Dye represents more than 30 NFL players, including Pro Bowlers Keith Brooking and Garrison Hearst. Garrison's mother, Mary, describes him like this: "Pat has a great gift of dealing with people. He's one of the few agents who came into our house and made us feel comfortable. That's important, because you are recruiting the parents as much as the player. He's always in our thoughts."

There are things that Pat Dye, Jr., learned from his father "the coach" and from his father "the parent" that have led this younger namesake to the top of his field. The work ethic his father instilled allowed him to leave an already successful career with an established company to create his own business. He credits his father's belief of setting lofty goals for making that business a success. But since he was brought up with the philosophy that life is not all business, he has also created a loving, caring home life.

Pat Dye, Sr., was an All-American collegiate football player with the University of Georgia and a National Coach of the Year for NCAA Division I schools at Auburn. He coached the Tigers for 12 years, believed in training both on and off the field and instilled that ethic into both his teams and his son.

"I think if there was one virtue or lesson that my father taught me above all else, it was to work hard," says Pat, Jr. "On the practice field he taught his athletes that there were certain things that were beyond their control. You cannot control how much ability you were born with, but if you outwork someone, you have every opportunity to reach or surpass their level of achievement." In the always rough and tumble, sometimes cutthroat world of professional sports agenting, hard work is a necessity. Having started his business in the basement of his home a decade earlier and now looking over the Atlanta skyline from his spacious office, it appears the hard work has paid off for the younger Dye.

The mindset that no obstacles are too high nor any challenge too tough are also bedrock in the teachings of his father. "My father took his first head coaching job at East Carolina University in 1974. He left for ECU from an assistant coaching job under Coach Bear Bryant at the University of Alabama the day after the team competed for the national championship against Notre Dame. Alabama was pretty much the pinnacle of his profession. When he reached ECU, it had terrible facilities and a stadium that seated 20,000. They had never beaten major Division I teams, but he loved the challenge. It was not long before they were beating Virginia, North Carolina and other ACC schools that had not offered his players scholarships. He used a formula and a regimen to overcome adversity and to create a winning tradition. He made the best with what he had, and he succeeded. He felt that you should have a plan to reach high goals so that even if you fall short, you will still achieve a very high level of success.

"After my father had great success at ECU and the University of Wyoming, he took the head coaching job at Auburn in 1981. At that point they had not beaten Alabama, their biggest rival, in close to ten years. So of course at the first press conference they asked him how long it would take to beat the Tide and he answered, "Sixty minutes," – the length of a regulation college football game. The reporters thought he was being cute, but this really just exemplified his attitude. He knew that only with a maximum effort for 60 minutes could they win. To beat the best, they had to play their best for all 60 minutes of the game."

But Pat, Sr., also had a completely different, very fatherly side. Pat, Jr., credits his tough-minded, hard-working father with being a solid emotional influence in his life and a paternal role model. "He taught me that being emotional was all right. I saw him cry in front of his team on a number of occasions. It showed how much he cared and how much passion he had for them. I thought that was pretty neat."

And even with the rigors and demands of being a head coach, Pat, Sr., always spent time with his son. "No matter how busy he was, he always tried to make time for me. He took me on trips other kids weren't taken on. He taught me how to hunt and fish. I can't tell you how much I looked forward to those times as a kid. The night before, it was hard to sleep, like Christmas morning. That is how I want my son to remember our time together and how I want to live my life with my family."

Pat Dye, Sr. taught quite a bit to his son about balance in life. During his youth he showed his son that a man could reach the top of his profession in a time-consuming career yet be a caring, present father. He told him that he needed goals, toughness and hard work to be successful, but he let him know that it was okay to be emotional as well. Perhaps above all, Pat's father showed him how to be a great father to his own children and gave him the tools to help reach that goal. The blueprint seems to have worked pretty effectively.

CHRIS EVERT

"If you can react the same way to winning and losing, that is a big accomplishment. That quality is important because it stays with you the rest of your life." These words were spoken by **CHRIS EVERT**, who has lived and practiced them both on and off the tennis court.

Born on December 21, 1954, in Fort Lauderdale, Florida, Christine Marie Evert was the daughter of a noted tennis player, her father Jimmy. She began taking lessons from him very early, and her style evolved rapidly to feature a powerful two-hand backhand and a degree of concentration that often unnerved opponents. At age 15, she beat top-ranked Margaret Smith Court, and in 1971 she became the youngest player to reach the semifinals of the U.S. Open championship. The following year she advanced to the semifinal round of her first Wimbledon tournament and won the Virginia Slims tournament.

In December 1972, Evert turned professional; she won her first professional tournament in March 1973 and graduated from high school soon after. Victories in the 1974 French championship and at Wimbledon highlighted a remarkable 56-match winning streak. Between 1975 and 1978 she won four consecutive U.S. Open titles. In 1976 she won her second Wimbledon title. Overall she won 18 Grand Slam tournaments (Wimbledon, French Open, Australian Open and U.S. Open) and 157 tour events.

Following her retirement in 1989, she became a television commentator, a special advisor to the United States National Tennis Team, and president of the Women's Tennis Association (1982-91). She also founded Chris Evert Charities, a not-for-profit organization that raises funds for innovative programs to improve the development and life outcomes of children, preserve and strengthen families, and promote healthy, drug-free behavior in society. Over the last decade, Chris Evert has raised more than $11 million to support the Ounce of Prevention Fund of Florida, the Drug Abuse Foundation of Palm Beach County, and their ongoing campaigns against drug-abuse and child neglect in South Florida.

In 1985 the Women's Sports Foundation named Evert the greatest woman athlete in the past 25 years. Among her other honors were the Women's Tennis Association Award (1992) and induction into the International Tennis Hall of Fame (1995).

She is married to ex-Olympic skier Andy Mill; they have three sons and live in Boca Raton, FL.

My father was the one tennis coach I ever had.

He grew up in Chicago and used to watch tennis legend Bill Tilden. After school Dad would go to the Armory downtown and watch them play, and he'd ballboy for all the pros that played there. His parents did not get him involved, and I am not sure how he became interested in tennis, but his fascination started it in our family. He hung out and then began to play. He grew up playing on those really fast indoor boards. He was one of the top junior players, got a scholarship and then went on to become the No. 1 singles player at the University of Notre Dame. He won the United States Indoor Championship, the Canadian Championship, and was a very formidable player until he got drafted into the Navy. He did his tour and returned home to earn a living, but there was very little money in playing tennis. But he went down to Fort Lauderdale and started, almost as a summer job, *teaching* tennis.

He came from a Depression-era family that was lower middle-class. He realized that tennis could open some doors. It got him a scholarship to a dream school, with a major in economics, and allowed him to become tops on the tennis team. He wanted that same thing for his kids.

We really had no choice as to whether we would play or not. He just started taking us over to Holiday Park, the public courts where he taught, when I was in kindergarten at the age of six. He started by throwing balls out of shopping carts. I remember feeling a little bit resentful because I used to like to play after school at my girlfriends' homes, going swimming and having barbecues. That quickly ended after I started going to the courts.

There are five kids in my family, and my older brother was already over there, so we had no choice in the matter. I never said, "No Dad, I don't want to go to Holiday Park." We were a little afraid of him anyway because he was very strict, and so we were kind of forced into doing it, but it turned out to be very lucky for me. Actually it worked out well for everyone in our family, because we all benefited from it in different ways.

He taught me to internalize things, whether good or bad. As I got older, I stopped doing so because it really is not that healthy. When I was young I was very serious, like my dad, rather than happy-go-lucky; my mom was really the balance. She is a lot of fun, but my dad was very hard working and all business. I remember him telling me at a very early age not to let your opponent see your emotions on the court. Never let them see what you are feeling because they can use it to their advantage. That turned out to be very successful advice for me at a young age, so I chose to live that way as well. Who knows if that was the real me? I am not sure. But it really helped my concentration, and that came from him. Concentration and a strong and hard work ethic were two things he really instilled in me.

We are pretty different as parents, mostly because I am the mom. He definitely was a strict father – there were boundaries and there were rules. I have kind of gone the other way – I'm a lot more easygoing with my kids. I let them express themselves and talk to me. Bad language is okay once in a while. I let them be themselves and be kids. I talk to them more, whereas my siblings and I were occasionally spanked. We had to be in bed every night at eight, and there were many more rules growing up. I went the other way because at times when I was young, I felt a little suppressed and frustrated with my parents' control over us. But it is interesting that Dad has mellowed a lot. He has come full circle and has actually felt uncomfortable when I have scolded my kids for arguing or something. He will say, "Oh, c'mon, they are just kids," and I will say, "What are you talking about?" It is just interesting that as much as I love and respect him, I have taken a different route in regard to raising my own children.

He was less hands-on with regard to my competitive tennis. He very rarely traveled to tournaments with me. He was never one of those parents that wanted to take any credit. He was out of the limelight and always remained humble. My mom and I always traveled together. He just did not like big crowds or the attention – if he went to Wimbledon, the cameras would be on him when I played. He would get claustrophobic when he was around a lot of people. He opted to stay home with the kids and become Mr. Mom. My mother traveled to Europe with me. But the most defining moment with my dad was when I won Wimbledon, when it was televised with a tape delay; I called to tell him I'd won, and I heard his voice break and him cry. Sometimes during those conversations after Grand Slam tournaments, we would both be crying on the phone. I would always call him when I won, but he would always tell me that win or lose, he was proud of me. Just to make that phone call was what I looked forward to. I could not wait to get off the court and talk to him.

He never played favorites. Something my mother once told me about my dad has stuck with me my whole life. He told her, "Even though Chrissie is No. 1 in the world, I am just as proud of Drew, Claire and John for receiving scholarships, becoming No. 1 on their respective teams, and for (my sister) Jeannie being top 10 in the U.S. women's rankings." He always treated everybody the same. After I won Wimbledon, I still had to fold the laundry, empty the dishwasher and make my bed. We did not change. That tells a lot about him and my mother both. Believe me, I had my moments and I was by no means perfect. I made mistakes and had my wild moments but I have stayed relatively grounded, and I think my dad played a big part in making a difference.

My relationship now with my father is fantastic. I was and still remain a daddy's girl. I never went through a period where I hated him, did not want to have anything to do with him or rebelled against him. Consequently, when I was around 18, all those rules and boundaries from my youth were dropped and he gave me all the freedom I could ever want. If he had been on my back, traveling with me every minute, had been critical of my tennis and been an overbearing parent, I probably would have rebelled. But he gave me so much space that I wanted to come back and wanted to talk with him all the time. I called him every day when I was on the tour, and nowadays I see him three times a week. He lives half an hour away, and because he and my mother still have a great relationship, we get together all the time.

I have been really lucky with that part of my life. So many of my friends are estranged from their parents, do not talk with them, or live 3000 miles away. I feel extremely fortunate.

TIMOTHY, CHRISTOPHER, ROBERT, STEVE FORBES & MOIRA FORBES MUMMA

MALCOLM FORBES lived an exciting and memorable life. He could be described in many ways: *bon vivant*, *raconteur*, balloonist, columnist, millionaire and – perhaps with most pride for him – father. He had five children who all adored him and whose affection he most definitely returned.

Daughter Moira remembers, "His greatest joys came in doing things he loved, and he wanted nothing less for the five of us. He used to say, 'My kids are my best friends. I think we are good friends of theirs. My wife and I never took the attitude that they owed us for having been born and having raised them.'

"He was right. And because he never thought I owed him anything, I was free to give, or really to return to him, with his own brand of total joy and enthusiasm, both his love and his affirmation. In all that I have, in all that I am, and in all that I do, he's there and he always will be there, and I'm *very* glad and *very* grateful."

Son Timothy recalls his father as an outdoorsman with a message beyond the will to balloon just for the sake of ballooning. "When we were on the Friendship Trip to China, the night before he made his balloon flight over

Beijing, he and I had one of our more animated discussions. You see, he didn't have permission to do it. His request had been denied by our Chinese hosts on the grounds of national security, no less. And I was arguing, 'No, you can't!' And he was saying, 'Yes, I must!' I didn't understand then why it was so important to him.

"But the next morning, sure enough, he took off. And to the profound dismay of the gathered officials, the tether line fell to the ground and the friendship balloon floated away, free. It landed about 20 minutes later – smack in the middle of a Red Army base. National security, indeed! That base is the reason permission had been denied in the first place.

"Pop and I spent a good hour or so together in a small room on that base while Chinese officials decided what to do about it – and of more immediate concern, what to do with us. Finally, with great wisdom and good grace, they apparently concluded that the whole thing never happened. We returned to the hotel, and not another word was said about it.

"But Pop couldn't and wouldn't let it go at that. There was a purpose to what he'd done, and he had to make sure everyone understood it. It was very simple, really. And that night at the farewell banquet he explained, 'What we did today, it wasn't to be naughty or unfriendly. It was to demonstrate the sport of ballooning. A balloon is not meant to be tied down. It's meant to be free, to float with the wind.'

"You see, for Pop, a balloon was the most apt symbol of the human spirit."

Christopher Forbes was touched by a certain moment his father shared with him in the heat of their conducting the family business.

"One never knew what to expect when walking into Pop's office. Early one day he called me in to empty 'my bucket' – his term for the folders of things he wanted to go over with us, which he kept in a file cabinet next to his desk. It was the usual miscellany: 'Did *I* approve this?', eyebrows arching as he handed me the bill for an acquisition for one of the art collections. Or, 'What can we *do* about this guy?', looking at a salesman's call report outlining our difficulties with one of our competitors. Or, 'How much should we give to this?', an invitation to a dinner at which one of his friends or colleagues was being honored. Or, pointing to a recent arrival from the framers, 'Where shall we hang this?' And so on. As I was getting up to go, he casually handed me a page proof from the galleys of his new book. In a gesture typical of the unexpected and wonderful things he loved to surprise us all with, he had written:

> *To my son Christopher*
> *Whose friendship, love, genius and wit*
> *Have been instrumental*
> *In making this life*
> *'More than I dreamed.'*

"I cried then, and when I think of it I try not to cry again."

Robert Forbes loved his father's touch of mirth, ease of laughter, and the epigrams which his father had everywhere. Age only matters if you are a wine. If you can't take it with you, I'm not going. "Talk about positive attitude!" Wealth is in the heart, not in the wallet. If the dinner check's delayed, try leaving. "I've been with him when he pulled that one. It works." Fun is not as much unless shared. When you are old enough for no one to say not to eat all the sweets you want, you do. "He sure did that. In the office after his passing, on one of his secretaries desks, I saw a typed-out recipe for Rice Krispie Treats with Peanut Butter." As you get older, don't slow down. Speed up. There's less time left. "Also seen in the office was a letter asking him what color he wanted his new Lamborghini Diablo." And on a plaque in the kitchen: He who dies with the most toys wins. "I think he got the blue ribbon here."

Probably the best known of the clan is Steve Forbes, who followed in his father's footsteps in his love of politics and desire to hold the highest office – a dream which thus far has not come to pass.

"When he was dealt a setback, he would initially look as if he had been physically hit by a punch. He would take stock – and then move ahead as if nothing had happened. When he did look back on disappointments, it was always with good-natured humor. On his failure to win the governorship of New Jersey, for instance, he said, 'I was nosed out by a landslide.'

"He was incapable of ill will or of pining for what might have been. Grudges and grievances were never a part of this man's makeup. He genuinely believed that things turned out for the best.

"He was generous. As a parent, he had unbounded love for his children and his grandchildren. He gave away much money to many causes. In a great number of cases, the recipient never knew who was the benefactor. He wanted to share his numerous collections with others. He thought it would be 'neat' if people could see what turned him on about these items. But he didn't want a mere display. When he looked at a toy boat, for instance, he also saw waves and motion.

"After I went to work for *Forbes*, I began to write editorials for the magazine. Inevitably, I would occasionally want to express opinions that differed rather sharply from his. He would argue with me, but if I stuck to my guns, he would smile and shake his head. 'Okay. It's *your* name that's on this.' Occasionally he would say, 'You've convinced me. I've changed my mind.' I would be on the clouds for the rest of the week. His philosophy was to allow me, and eventually my brothers and sister, enough latitude to learn from our mistakes, but not to be destroyed by them.

"No matter what he did, no matter how impressive the achievement in business, ballooning, writing, motorcycling, entertaining and collecting, we knew that as long as he lived the best was always yet to come. Now he is gone. But in a larger, truer sense, death has not triumphed, and if we follow, as he did, the better angels of our nature, it never will."

BRUCE S. GORDON

BRUCE GORDON is president of the Retail Markets Group, responsible for consumer and small business customers, for Verizon Communications, Inc. He also directs corporate advertising and brand management. Gordon began his career at Bell of Pennsylvania in 1968 as a management trainee and advanced through assignments in personnel, operations, and sales and marketing.

In July 2002 *Fortune* magazine named him to its "50 Most Powerful Black Executives" list as number six. Previously, *Black Enterprise* magazine named Bruce Gordon "1998 Executive of the Year." He is a member of the board of the Advertising Council, Inc., Bartech Personnel Services, Office Depot, The Southern Company and Tyco International, Ltd. He is also a member of the Executive Leadership Council. Gordon is a trustee of Gettysburg College, the Alvin Ailey Dance Foundation and Lincoln Center. Born in Camden, New Jersey, he received a B.A. from Gettysburg College and received an M.S. from the Massachusetts Institute of Technology as an Alfred P. Sloan Fellow.

My dad's impact on me and its relevance to my life is very much tied to my ethnicity. First of all, my father was all about education. He had an undergraduate degree from what was then known as Glasboro State Teachers College, and he also had a masters degree from the University of Pennsylvania. This was in the 1930s when there were not a lot of African-Americans as educationally advanced as he was.

My father was also an activist in the NAACP from a civil rights perspective, and he was active in the teachers union because he was an educator. By the time he finished his career, he was a dean at Tampa County Community College. But the real breakthrough for him came as the first African-American junior high school principal in the state of New Jersey.

All this by a man who had once quit high school.

My father grew up in rural South New Jersey on a farm and worked as a laborer in an oil refinery. He also was a chef for a hunting lodge on the weekends. It was, overall, a varied but blue-collar, working-class upbringing.

He was a great cook. I know a lot of men who don't cook, but all the men in my family – my father, me and my son – are good cooks. My dad believed that men should do everything, that you should not be limited to conventional thinking in what you choose to pursue and do.

Here's a funny story about my dad: In my era, junior high school was from seventh to ninth grade. In Camden, New Jersey, where I grew up, it was an accepted fact that one particular coach was the best for junior high school athletics, and I aspired to play for him. Between my seventh and eighth grade years, my dad was promoted to principal of the junior high school. I came home one day and he said, "I have good news and bad news. The good news is I've been promoted from being an elementary school principal to being junior high school principal. That is a truly significant thing under any circumstances, but it is particularly noteworthy since I am African-American. The bad news is it's your junior high school. My guess is you probably won't want to go to the same school where your dad's the principal, so I've already made arrangements for you to go to the junior high school across town."

And I said, "Not a chance, because if I go to the junior high school across town, I won't be able to play for the best coach."

So we had to make up our minds to peacefully co-exist under the same schoolhouse roof. At the end of the day, he and I both survived and were better off for having done it.

Two things stand out when I think of my father. One is that he made it very clear to me that the only person who could limit my accomplishments was me. Regardless of the social climate and expectations of the day, he instilled in me the belief that I had all the gifts and talents necessary to do whatever I chose to do. He didn't want me to be limited by stereotypical career definitions. The word "impossible" was never part of our discussions, because anything and everything was achievable.

The second thing is that my father prided himself on being a well-rounded guy. He had significant stature in the community as an educator, but his pride led him to do other things as well to provide for his family. Here was a man who had a graduate degree from the University of Pennsylvania and was principal of a junior high school, but during the summers he took jobs as a laborer or worked night shifts in order to take care of his family.

He practiced what he preached: one, you can do whatever you want to do, and two, once you decide what you want to do, if you are willing to do whatever it takes to get there, then the world is yours. That whatever-it-takes attitude is something he instilled in me.

CHRISTIE HEFNER

CHRISTIE HEFNER oversees policy, management and strategy in all areas of Playboy Enterprises. She joined Playboy in 1975 and worked in a variety of the company's businesses before being named president in 1982. In 1988, she was elected to her present position of Chairman and CEO with the New York Stock Exchange-listed international media and entertainment company.

Besides directing Playboy Enterprises' operations, Hefner is active in a number of local and national organizations. She serves on the boards of *MarketWatch.com*, the Magazine Publishers Association, the Business Committee for the Arts, Canyon Ranch Health Resort, and on the board of governors of the Museum of Television & Radio Media Center. Hefner is also on the advisory boards of the American Civil Liberties Union, the Creative Coalition, and Advertising Women of New York, as well as a member of the Chicago Council on Foreign Relations and the National Cable & Telecommunications Association's Diversity Committee. She also spent four years as project board chairman for the CORE Center, raising $30 million to build this innovative clinic and research facility, which opened in Chicago in the summer of 1998. The CORE Center conducts clinical research and provides prevention education and outpatient care for people with HIV/AIDS and other communicable diseases.

As the first woman to receive the Executive Leadership Award from the National Society of Fundraising Executives, Hefner has been honored with a Humanitarian Award from the Rainbow/PUSH Coalition, the Spirit of Life Award from the City of Hope and the Corporate Leadership Award from the AIDS Pastoral Care Network. In 2002 she received the Committee of 200's Philanthropic Innovator Luminary Award and the National Cable & Telecommunications Association's Vanguard Award for Distinguished Leadership, the cable industry's highest honor, for her longstanding commitment to the First Amendment rights of cable programmers and operators and for her strong advocacy of workplace diversity. In 2003 she received the University of Illinois at Chicago's Family Business Council's Leadership Award, bearing an inscription recognizing her "vision, determination and courage in refocusing, diversifying and ultimately ensuring the future of an American icon, leading Playboy into the new millennium."

Hefner was born in Chicago in 1952. Elected to Phi Beta Kappa in her junior year of college, Hefner graduated from Brandeis University *summa cum laude* with a Bachelor of Arts degree in English and American literature in 1974. She became a President's Councilor of her alma mater in 1978.

She is married to real estate developer and attorney William A. Marovitz, a former Illinois state senator.

My parents divorced when I was very young, so I did not grow up living with my father. My mother also remarried when I was very young. I mostly lived with her, my brother and my stepfather in Wilmette, a suburb of Chicago, where my father was living at the time. My earliest interaction with him was through visits that we had for my birthday, his birthday, Christmas or other special occasions, as opposed to his being a day-in-day-out parent. We tended to celebrate with family dinners composed of his parents, my brother, and the two of us.

One of the things I remember most distinctly from all the years of growing up was his avid fondness for games. From very early on, after he bought and moved into the original Playboy Mansion here in

Chicago, he had a very elaborate game room. Not only was there a pool table and pinball machines, but he also had all the newest and most interesting video games as they came on the market. So, for a kid, being able to go somewhere and play games without having to put quarters in the machine was very cool.

One of the qualities that we share, and one that became evident even when I was a child, is that we are both extremely competitive. Whether it was pool or pinball or backgammon – which we both played a lot at certain periods – I always had a great desire to win. But just as much as winning, we both wanted to do our best. I do think that is secretly what drives many successful people.

I did not grow up expecting to go to work in the company, and I do not think it was in my father's game plan either. My interest in college was more toward journalism. I worked as a journalist after graduating and was getting ready to go to law school when I visited my father, who by then had moved to L.A. He raised the idea of my coming to work for the company. At that point, he has said in retrospect, he was not thinking long-term. He felt it would be a way for us to get closer and that I could learn a little bit about what he did. I would likely work for a few years in the company and then go to law school. It was an enormous advantage that there was never a grand plan for me to take over the business, because I did not have to go through the challenge of being introduced as the heir apparent.

In terms of moral values, my mother and father are very similar. They are also in line with my generation's political values. One of the things that was different for me growing up, compared to my contemporaries, was the whole absence of a generation gap in my family. Whether it was the war in Vietnam or attitudes about sex and marriage, both of my parents had points of view that were very unusual for their generation and much more typical of mine, the baby boomers. In many ways it is easy to see why my parents got married—although I think they got married too young—because they are very compatible in terms of their view of the world.

My father has not become cynical or jaded as he has become successful and powerful. His closest friends are people he has known his whole life. He does not feel the need to trade in his old friends for a group of hip, new powerful people.

We have some differences. His life and the magazine are inextricably linked. He is going to be working all of his life, and given that his mother lived to be 101, I think that is decades more. In that sense, I am less the visionary entrepreneur – personally tied up in the vision of the magazine and company – and more the CEO of the corporation. As a result, I do not envision myself working for the company for the rest of my life. I am a creative person in the business sense, because I am a creative problem solver and negotiator, but not in the way that my father is a creative genius. I do not have any idea for a world-changing new magazine. In part, what I try to do is create an environment where creative people can do great work, and I try to be strategically creative. You see this in the fact that we have moved from being a domestic publishing company to an international multi-media company.

Playboy reflects values that are dad's values because he really shaped it in his own image. These are things at which I work very hard to preserve. We place a premium on ethics and integrity in our business dealings. We have respect for individuals. We don't listen in on employees' phone conversations or have people take random drug tests or polygraph tests. Also, we have made a great commitment to diversity. My father actually quit one of his first jobs in the personnel department of a Chicago company when he was told not to bother interviewing people with Jewish or foreign-sounding last names. So it stood to reason that *Playboy* started with the notion that people would be hired and promoted based upon their abilities, not their age, their gender or their sexual orientation. These are the qualities and beliefs he maintains, along with a deep pride in the quality of the work and the magazine. It has also engendered a lot of pride in the people who have worked here over the years.

We both have been very politically active. Our political views, in terms of issues and candidates, are very similar. I started when I was a kid, going door to door for elected officials and candidates I believed in. Now as an adult, I am able to make use of the position that I have for greater good. It has included, for my father, starting the Playboy

Foundation and his own activities, which is, as he would say, putting your money where your mouth is. That is certainly something I grew up with and have emulated philanthropically, politically and in the arts. I am very proud of my father's charitable work and his activism.

One of the qualities he has that I do not have – at least not to the degree he does, but I find quite inspirational – is that he is 78 years old but he wakes up as excited about the day as he did when he was 22 years old. He has this boyish sense of joy about life and lives every day to the fullest. All of us say we behave in that manner, because it would be foolish to say otherwise, but I think very few people truly live that way. In terms of work, I am a little bit more driven to keep that sense of perspective.

Neither of us is a great phone correspondent, so I stay with him when I go to L.A., which is almost every month, and that is time we spend together kicking around ideas for work or just catching up. I remember when I became president and the company was facing a real financial crisis. We were really in the middle of a turnaround, and at one point I was out in L.A. updating my father on what was happening. He turned to me and said, "I want you to know that I sleep better at night knowing you are in the position that you are in." I told him how much I appreciated it and how hard I was working to make things better, and he said, "I know you are. I really believe it is going to be all right, but I want you to know that at the end of the day this is not the most important thing in life." In fact, the magazine and the business is one of the most important things to him, but it was his way of telling me not to lose sight of the difference between what you do for a living and living.

That is great advice.

ROBERT A. IGER

ROBERT A. IGER was named president and chief operating officer of The Walt Disney Company in January 2000. At that time he also became a member of Disney's board of directors and its executive management committee. Iger oversees all aspects of The Walt Disney Company's operations on a worldwide basis.

He is a member of the board of directors of Lincoln Center for the Performing Arts, Inc., and New York City Outward Bound. He is a trustee of the Museum of Television and Radio and of Ithaca College, where he graduated *magna cum laude.*

On October 1, 2005, Mr. Iger succeeded Michael Eisner as the CEO of The Walt Disney Company.

A native of New York, Iger was born February 10, 1951. He has four children and is married to television personality Willow Bay.

Bob Iger's apple did not fall far from the tree. He took his father's passions and vocation and amplified them to great heights. He credits his success in business and parenting and his moral certitude to his upbringing and his father's convictions.

"My father was in the advertising business on the agency side for many years. He grew up in Brooklyn, New York, and fought in World War II. He played professional jazz trumpet for a short period of time.

He went into publishing, mostly trade publications, and eventually became a teacher of marketing.

"Certainly throughout my childhood he was a devoted parent. He gave us tons of time, but he also respected us. I wouldn't say we were treated as adults, because that would not quite be right, but we were always part of the dinner table conversations. Our lives were definitely a focal point for my parents."

The conversations during the evenings were eclectic and wide ranging and started Iger on a course of great achievement.

"He had an intellectual curiosity – an insatiable appetite for information – and his interests were extremely varied. That, above all else, was the most meaningful thing my father gave to me.

"I was taught, in many respects, what to take seriously and what not to – what to let bother me and what not to let bother me. He gave me a sense that there are things in the world that are important and things that are not. A lot of it comes down to priority, of how you spend the time in your life, what drives or moves you and what does not or should not.

"This philosophy manifested itself with a political and social conscience that, above all, made him steadfast in his belief that you deal with people on equal ground and with veracity.

"He was very politically aware, and we grew up in a household that was political in the sense that he made us very aware of the issues of the day. Of course, civil rights was a primary one, and he implanted our values as it relates to that.

"One of the things that was a significant lesson or a teaching of sorts from my father was that there is no such thing as sacrifice when it comes to integrity. He taught me to treat people with respect and to be fair."

Iger oversees the second largest media conglomerate in the world. He lives in Los Angeles with his wife, a former high-fashion model and Ivy League graduate, and their children. He deals with some of the biggest names in Hollywood and most profitable companies on Wall Street. His escape is music – the music his father played for him.

"My musical side is in appreciation versus performance. It is both eclectic and fervent – I'm an avid music fan. I love jazz, particularly jazz ballads sung by Billie Holliday, Sarah Vaughan and Ella Fitzgerald. I also like classical and classic rock and a little bit of opera sprinkled in.

"My father's love for music, the fact that there was always music playing in our house, that it was always being talked about and that he considered it important, clearly had an influence on me. We used to go to summer jazz festivals. One of my fondest memories was hearing Duke Ellington and His Orchestra play in the early 1960s. It was July 4th in, of all places, Milwaukee."

Many things are passed through the years within families. Heirlooms, homes, wedding dresses and even names are handed down from parents to children. It is rare, though, when music, usually a divider in the "generation gap," links not only two but three generations.

"I have shared my love of music that my father passed to me with my grown daughters. They like jazz, and it's not typical that you'll find a 26- and 23-year-old listening to Louis Armstrong and Ella Fitzgerald duets. That would be a favorite of theirs, but I also raised them on Beatles music, which has made them devoted Beatles fans. I suspect that a lot of people from my generation, having grown up with the Beatles, passed their love along to their children. We also listened to a lot of folk music like Peter, Paul and Mary, and I think they very much attribute their love of music to me and what I exposed them to growing up.

"Interestingly enough, my father is still somewhat active in jazz circles in New York and belongs to a group called 'Jazz at Noon,' which has been in existence for decades. It's a bunch of former jazz musicians who became businessmen and get together and play every Friday afternoon. They've moved from place to place in New York over the years. Not that long ago, he and my 23-year-old daughter went together. They play music during lunch, and I have gone with him myself on many occasions."

JESSE JACKSON, JR.

REP. JESSE L. JACKSON, JR., began service in the United States House of Representatives on December 12, 1995, as he was sworn in as a member of the 104th Congress, the 91st African-American ever elected to Congress.

Prior to his congressional service, Rep. Jackson served as the National Field Director of the National Rainbow Coalition.

Born in the midst of the voting rights struggle on March 11, 1965, Jackson spent his twenty-first birthday in a jail cell in Washington, D.C., for taking part in a protest at the South African Embassy against apartheid. He also demonstrated weekly in front of the South African Consulate in Chicago. Jackson was on stage with Nelson Mandela during his historic speech following a 27-year imprisonment in Cape Town.

Jackson graduated *magna cum laude* from North Carolina A & T State University in Greensboro, North Carolina, with a B.S. in business management. Three years later, he earned a Master of Arts degree in theology from the Chicago Theological Seminary, and in 1993 he received his juris doctorate from the University of Illinois College of Law. Jackson has co-authored *A More Perfect Union: Advancing New American Rights* (2001) with Frank E. Watkins. He has also co-authored *Legal Lynching* (1996), *Legal Lynching II* (2001), and *It's*

About the Money (1999).

Rep. Jackson resides in the Second Congressional District of Illinois with his wife Sandi, daughter Jessica Donatella and son Jesse L. Jackson, III.

Most of my life I knew there was something special about my father, because everyone knew who I was before I knew them. "Hey, that's Jesse Jackson's son," was a common refrain. It was not really until my latter, more conscious years that I began to reflect upon his mission, his work, the implications, the process for change in America and how valuable his contribution has been.

One of the first things I've had to come to terms with about being who I am is that I inherited my father's friends and his detractors, neither of which I have earned. So I have to work extremely hard to move the detractors into the friends category and to earn his friends as my own, legitimately and independently of his relationships with them. It's hard to convince people you are who you are, and I have spent the last eight years in public life confronting this problem. My last opponent for Congress was a 70-year-old guy named Jesse Jackson! The theme of his campaign was, "He ran on his daddy's name; why can't I? I had the name before him and his daddy."

It never ends. I'm a 40-year-old but I'm still a kid. You're always riding the coattails. I've got two kids and a wife of my own, pay my own taxes, but to some I'll never be my own man.

In 1984 when my father was running for President, I flew one weekend with him to Iowa. Iowa is such a clearly beautiful state when you look at it while flying over it. You can see everyone's farms in parcels, everyone's property. Dad said, "You know, son, when you're flying high you can miss a lot of details."

That lesson has taken so many turns and meanings in my life. That is, when you have high name recognition, sometimes you do not get to develop genuine friendships. When you are well known, sometimes you are approached by people who have ulterior motives.

I have always admired, respected and on some levels worshipped my father. I've seen him in that omnipotent light. Growing up, no one could tell me there was anything wrong with him. But when I was in seminary and started thinking a lot more critically, I began to evaluate my relationships, including the one with my father. I have seen the human side of him that I have come to wrestle with. Are these traits that I will emulate? If you accept your parents completely, uncritically, which I did for a very long time, you end up being little versions of them, so I've tried to look at things objectively, deal with it the best I possibly can, and I think my wife likes the man I have become.

On the balance sheet of life, obviously being the son of my father has helped more than it has hurt. But it's all a function of how you handle it. I grew up with children whose parents read like a virtual who's who that have not handled it well, from my perspective. My father used to speak at high schools, and he used to say, "Down with dope, up with hope." Now, do I need to go try dope to figure out from an experiential point of view if my father is right? The answer is obviously no. It was good, solid, parental advice that he was giving at home but also to other students across the country. I've seen Rev. Jackson in action, and even as an adult I try to emulate some of that courage.

Like George Foreman, I named my daughter Jessica and I named my son Jesse III. When I see Jessica, she clearly reflects her grandfather's energy and zeal. She is like a three-year-old going on 12. She's very thoughtful. I had to reflect long and hard on whether or not to name my son Jesse. I don't know if I want him to assume the responsibility or to not have the opportunity to enjoy some level of anonymity without having to live up to his grandfather or his father. My wife and I settled on the idea that at the appropriate time we would choose a nickname for him, to give him a chance to make a few mistakes in life.

Sometimes lessons are taught through actions and not through advice. One thing I learned from watching my father is that not all of life is achieving vertical growth, a lot of it is horizontal, and sometimes when you are trying to get from point A to the moon, you should just be moving horizontally to point B. This has served me well in politics.

Since I've been in Congress, I have heard I should run for mayor, for U.S. Senate, even for the Presidency. I've been told, "You can be the first black this and the first black that." But what I have focused on is helping other people in my age group get elected, and thus I've spent my time building a base horizontally. I'm not running from the 2nd District of Illinois to the Senate or the White House or something else, but running directly to people and trying to establish relationships.

The same thing works with exposure. When I was in business school, we used to talk about diminishing laws. How many vanilla milk shakes can you drink before you don't want any more vanilla milk shakes? How many press conferences can you call before people turn around and say, "I do not want to see that guy anymore"? My father has been in the spotlight for many years, and it has served him and a generation of people very well, but as a politician I am not totally convinced it would serve the same purpose for me. As an elected official, I have to measure what issues I choose and how often people see me. I want to have some reasonable control over my future, because at 48 I do not want to have saturated the public consciousness with myself. I will be a relatively young man in politics. If I am not careful, people could become tired of me.

I guess the earliest recollection of my father was that he was always busy and was not at home as often as I would have liked. Every Saturday we would go to what was then known as "Operation Bread Basket" (now "Operation Push"), where he has delivered a speech for the last 35 years. It's called the Saturday forum, and it is where he talks about contemporary issues. After "Push" in the mornings, in the afternoon my brother and I would get in a car and drive to O'Hare Airport, where we would see him off to other speaking engagements and travels.

Just last week before he left for a trip to Thailand, we were sitting out in my backyard and talking about how much fun I have with my daughter Jessica, how I take her to the zoo and stuff like that. It was a special moment for me as he said, "Wow, I really wish I had that kind of time to spend with you when you were growing up." It was a rare moment for both of us because I told him, "There's no better time than the present." It was his way of telling me and my acknowledging that he has made enormous sacrifices. I responded by saying, "Indeed, that enormous sacrifice has produced a congressman, an MBA and successful businessman, a lawyer and two wonderful daughters. We are the sum total of our experiences."

For almost 20 years I have been a surrogate speaker for my father whenever he could not make an engagement. For the first time, at the age of 38, I have asked him to make appearances when I cannot. We have a mutual respect and caring for each other like at no other time in our lives. That is a heck of a good position to be in.

CORETTA SCOTT KING

April 27, 1927 – January 30, 2006

"I think, on many points, she educated me. When I met her, she was very concerned about the things we are trying to do now. I never will forget the first discussion we had on the whole question of racial injustice and economic injustice and the question of peace. In her college days she had been actively engaged in movements dealing with these problems. I wish I could say, to satisfy my masculine ego, that I led her down this path; but I must say we went down it together, because she was as actively involved and concerned when we met as she is now."

That is how Martin Luther King, Jr., described his wife shortly before his death in 1968.

CORETTA SCOTT KING was one of America's most influential women leaders. Prepared by her family, education and personality for a life committed to social justice and peace, she entered the world stage in 1955 as wife of the Reverend Dr. Martin Luther King, Jr., and as a participant in the American Civil Rights Movement. Her remarkable partnership with Dr. King resulted not only in four talented children, but also in a life devoted to the highest values of human dignity in service to social change. Mrs. King has traveled throughout the world speaking out on behalf of racial and economic justice, women's and children's rights, gay and lesbian dignity, religious freedom, the needs of the poor and homeless, full employment, health care, educational opportunities, nuclear disarmament and ecological sanity. In her distinguished career, she lent her support to democracy movements worldwide and served as a consultant to many world leaders, including Corazon Aquino, Kenneth Kaunda and Nelson Mandela.

It is a wonder that my father did not end up in a swamp because of his obvious self-respect. His additional and unforgivable crime was that he worked too hard and got ahead – ahead of some poor whites. When he and my mother were married, he had a steady job in one of the local sawmills earning three dollars a day. By the time I was born, he had saved enough money to buy a truck and was hauling logs and timber for the local sawmill operator. He had also learned the barber's trade, and in the evenings and on weekends there might be a line of men outside our house waiting to have their hair cut. Mother would help him by also cutting hair when there were more customers than my father could handle.

Because of the Depression, he began what was called "truck farming." On our piece of land we raised corn, peas, potatoes and garden vegetables. We had hogs, cows and chickens. My father hired someone to plow the fields, but we planted the corn, hoed it and gathered it, fed the chickens and hogs and milked the cows. We did not sell the produce – we and the animals ate it. Even if we had not needed it, living on a farm without growing things was unthinkable.

So we all worked, but Daddy worked harder than almost anyone for miles around. While both my parents shared the feeling that we must learn how to work, my father seemed to have a passion for keeping busy. He used to chide us about getting up early, saying, "When I was growing up at home, we ate breakfast every morning by lamplight. If you don't have anything to do, just get up and sit down. I won't have lazy people in my house."

Although (because of outstanding debts) he got no money to take home from his regular job, my father derived some income from hauling lumber for other people on weekends and sometimes during the night. But even this got him into trouble with the poor whites. He was the only black who owned a truck. This brought him into competition with the whites, and they resented him. Sometimes they would stop him on a lonely road and curse him and threaten to kill him – and there was always a good chance they might do it. He was not a big man, only about five feet seven, but he had a lot of courage. He never ran away, and I am sure that is why he survived. He would stand up to them quietly and respectfully.

I learned very early in life to live with fear for the people I loved. It was good training, for I lived that way most of my life. My father, in his bravery and his refusal to be beaten down, is very much the same kind of man my husband was.

My father is such an amazing person. He never became bitter, despite all the incidents, all the humiliations and harassment by the whites who wanted to keep him down because they saw their own jobs imperiled, and because they did not want any black man to rise above "his place."

Yet, my father would say, "There are some good white folks." Many years later people accepted him as a substantial person, and he could say, "Nobody hates me. I have paid all my debts. My credit is good. That is because of the way I have conducted myself. I haven't an enemy in the world." And it was true. I know his example helped me not to hate.

EVERETT RAYMOND KINSTLER

KINSTLER, America's foremost portraiturist, has painted more than 500 portraits of such well known personalities as Tony Bennett, Carol Burnett, Peter O'Toole, James Cagney, Betty Ford, Gene Hackman, Katharine Hepburn, Lady Bird Johnson, Paul Newman, Gregory Peck, John Wayne; astronauts Alan Shepard and Scott Carpenter; Supreme Court Justices Harry Blackmun and Ruth Bader Ginsburg; writers Tennessee Williams and Tom Wolfe; sports figures Arthur Ashe and Byron Nelson; six U.S. governors; four U.S. Secretaries of State; and the presidents of colleges and universities, including Brown, Harvard, Princeton, Smith, Wellesley, Williams and Yale.

Five Presidents have posed for him: Nixon, Ford, Reagan, Bush and Clinton. His portraits of Ford and Reagan are the official White House portraits. Kinstler has painted more than 50 U.S. cabinet officers, more than any artist in the country's history.

The National Portrait Gallery in Washington, D.C. has acquired more than 50 of his works for its permanent collection. Kinstler is represented in the Metropolitan Museum of Art, Brooklyn Museum, and the Butler Institute of American Art, among others. In 1999 Kinstler received the Copley Medal from the Smithsonian National Portrait Gallery, the highest award the gallery bestows on a portrait artist.

Raymond Kinstler's father was born before the turn of the 20th century, served in World War I and had a job with his family's textiles company for his entire working life. He hated it. Kinstler grew up in Manhattan, a Depression-era kid, as an only child to his very devoted parents. "From a very early age my father noticed I had a marked interest, and fair, to say, a talent for drawing. I used to copy comic strips from the newspapers and photographs from illustrated magazines, so it was pretty clear that art was going to be a big part of my life. My dream was to be an illustrator for *The Saturday Evening Post*.

"I was an honor student at The School for Music and Art in the city. In order to attend, you had to have artistic talent and also achieve a high academic level. After my first year there, I was very unhappy and transferred to a trade school. I wanted to earn a living, and the trade school was teaching me how I might earn one through art. For example, they might have given me an assignment to draw a wristwatch advertisement for a newspaper or magazine. It was so important for me to do something with my abilities because I was just not happy in school.

"I have spoken to many actors over the years, and they describe the same calling that I had for art at the early age of 11 or 12 that drew them to the theater. So as I turned 15 and became more and more unhappy – although I remained a good kid and top student – I answered an ad for an inker. Another artist would pencil in a comic strip, then an apprentice (or inker) would fill in the lines with ink. So I went to see a man at 45th street at a company called Cinema Comics, and I was interviewed by an editor who offered me a job at fifteen dollars for a six-day week. I then went to my father and asked for his permission. As I reflect back on this many decades later, I wonder how my father would ever allow me to leave school. This was not an era when kids took off a year to 'go find themselves.' The only time a child left school was for deprivation reasons – if the parents were handicapped or incapacitated, it might be necessary for the child to earn money to assist. The best answer I can come up with is twofold. I think my father loved me and he saw in me a kid who was talented, who loved to draw, and he himself was in a family business which he despised. In addition, Dad saw a boy who was a good, motivated kid who had no problems other than that he was unhappy in school. So my father told me to take the job with his blessing, and he said one thing I remember particularly. He told me, 'You're a lucky young man because you will be able to earn your living doing something you love and enjoy all your life. Don't you ever forget it.' And truly I never did.

"Recently I was painting a portrait of the retiring chairman of the Federal Reserve Bank of New York. He and I discussed our chosen professions and we agreed that anyone who has a passion for what they do has been truly blessed.

"My five daughters, who had all the educational opportunities afforded to them, say to me, 'We envy you,' and they tell me, 'You knew what you wanted to do all your life and you followed it.' And they're right. Not a day goes by that I do not thank my father for his love and encouragement."

SALLIE KRAWCHECK

As Chairman and Chief Executive Officer of Smith Barney, **SALLIE L. KRAWCHECK** oversees global management of one of the four key businesses of parent company Citigroup. She is responsible for more than 500 offices and 23,000 employees around the world. She is also a member of the Citigroup Management and Business Heads Committees and the Citigroup Foundation Board, as well as its Business Practices Committee.

A native of Charleston, South Carolina, Krawcheck attended the University of North Carolina at Chapel Hill on the prestigious Morehead Scholarship, and graduated in 1987 with academic honors and a Bachelor of Arts degree. In 1992 she received a Master of Business degree from Columbia University. She is also a member of the Board of Directors for the University of North Carolina at Chapel Hill Foundations, Inc., and the Board of Overseers for Columbia Business School. In 2003 Krawcheck was named *Fortune* magazine's Most Influential Person Under the Age of 40 and was again one of its "Most Powerful Women." In 2002 she was named one of *Time* magazine's "Global Business Influentials."

❧

It was a fairly big jump from the small city of Charleston, South Carolina, to the financial capital of the world, New York City. But Sallie Krawcheck has reached the pinnacle of her profession at a startlingly young age. "On the first day of my first job in New York City at one of the big brokerage firms, I saw a man have a heart attack out of the corner of my eye. When I told my dad, his first reaction was, 'Good Lord, I'll come and get you.' But he had prepared me for life in Manhattan by instilling self-confidence at a young age, combined with the comfort of knowing he would hop on a plane to retrieve me at a moment's notice."

After the various "book-cooking" scandals of the late 1990s, honesty and credibility were as important as making money in the philosophy of Wall Street players. Krawcheck was brought in as CEO of Smith Barney by the CEO of Citigroup, the parent company, because of her impeccable reputation.

"When our family would break house rules, punishment was swift. There were some givens in the family, and the givens were the absolute highest level of integrity. We were expected, since our parents gave us the gift of education, to achieve to the highest level with the highest standards."

Prior to the women's movement of the 1970s, young women didn't always have the same opportunities for career advancement that men had. But Krawcheck's home life prepared her for any eventuality.

"Growing up in the South in the '60s and '70s, my parents never made me feel like my brothers could do things that I couldn't. In fact, I was in an all-girls school, and when my grades began to fall, my father and mother did not hesitate to pull me out and put me in another school, one that was co-ed and had tougher academic requirements. They made the decision that I was bored at my previous school and never blinked an eye about whether I could handle it at the new school. And they were right in their confidence. I went from Cs to first in the class in my first trimester at the new school.

"The way my father gave me the confidence to reach high goals was brilliant. He did it so matter-of-factly. He never sat me down and said, 'Honey, you can really go everywhere and do everything.' What he did was mention it in passing, as though it were just the truth. He would provide subtle reminders like, 'You can do anything you put your mind to,' or, 'Isn't it great that you have the brain you have,' and, 'You have such wonderful abilities.' When I was teased by the other girls at school, which happened a good bit, he convinced me that it was because they were jealous of my ability and talent.

"Because it was so hard to get noticed in a family of six, the one sure way to get attention was to bring home good grades. It was in this way that I received such positive reinforcement, and because my dad encouraged me so nonchalantly, it never occurred to me until my early twenties that he might be overly optimistic with regard to me. But by that point the foundation had been laid, and I was off doing my own thing.

"My father believed in providing my siblings and me with a certain amount of personal attention. Often times it was difficult to do this with four children so similar in age, but he would do little things for each of us. For instance, one of my most vivid memories of my dad is going to the fair with him. At some point he promised he would get me a balloon – not my brothers, but me. I was to get the only one. But early in the day it started to pour rain and we ran to the car. I started to bawl because I had no balloon. But the image etched in my brain is of my father walking (and it's become a several mile, uphill-both-ways walk in my memory) through the rain, soaked to the skin, with wet foggy glasses, approaching the car with a red balloon just for me. It taught me that when you make a promise, you keep a promise, no matter how uncomfortable that may be.

"It also emphasized that you treat each child a little bit differently. At the fair my father gave each of us something individual. One of us got a stuffed animal, one went on a special ride, one had cotton candy and, of course, I got the balloon. He tried to find something unique for each kid. Now I try to do things like take individual weekends with each of my children in order to spend one-on-one time with them.

"He also taught me that you could have fun with your kids and have a good time as a parent. Every night when he came home, he would have a race up the stairs with the five of us. Now, I'm not sure how we did it, since the stairs are quite narrow, but clearly there was some manhandling going on. Or we would go to the beach and he would always bodysurf with us. He took us sailing. In that age, parents were parents and children were children, but we still managed to have a lot of good times – good memories.

"But the primary gift, as I step back and think about the biggest way he influenced my siblings and me, was that he had a rock solid belief in the value of education. He sacrificed so much to send us all to school. My hometown of Charleston historically did not have the strongest public education in the country. My mother and father were married when they were quite young, in their early twenties, and they proceeded to have four children in three years and 11 months – and there were no twins in there. My siblings and I were born when dad was in law school, and then he went into the South Carolina legislature, which does not pay very much.

"Despite not having much money, he took out loans upon loans to send us to private schools. Despite their being well off presently, dad actually was paying off those loans, in some cases, into our thirties. So that was the sacrifice he made, which made the meaningful difference in each of our lives. It turned out pretty well, because in addition to myself, I have three siblings who all graduated from law school."

SHELLY LAZARUS

SHELLY LAZARUS, Chairman and Chief Executive Officer for Ogilvy & Mather Worldwide, has been working "in the business I love" for more than three decades. She studied psychology as an undergraduate at Smith College and then earned an MBA in marketing from Columbia University. She became CEO of Ogilvy & Mather in 1996 and Chairman in 1997.

Advertising Women of New York named her Advertising Woman of the Year in 1994. She was a recipient of Women in Communications' Matrix Award in 1995 and was named Business Woman of the Year by the New York City Partnership in 1996. She has been listed in *Fortune* magazine's annual ranking of the 50 Most Powerful Women in American Business since its inception in 1998. And most recently, she was given Columbia Business School's Distinguished Leadership Award in Business, the first woman to be so honored.

Lazarus serves on the boards of a number of business, philanthropic and academic institutions, including General Electric, Ann Taylor Stores, New York Presbyterian Hospital, American Museum of Natural History, Columbia University Business School, The September 11th Fund and the World Wildlife Fund. She has also served as chairman of the leading industry trade group, the American Association of Advertising Agencies — only one of two women to do so.

She is married to Dr. George Lazarus, a New York pediatrician, and is mother to their three children, who range in age from 15 to 29.

My father was a CPA and grew up in New York. My grandfather was a successful manufacturer of pillows and blankets – anything made with feathers and down. Much to the chagrin of my grandfather, at the age of 18 my father said he wanted to go to college and did not want to work in the family business. He had just met my mother and was going to go off with her and set out on his own. He went to City College of New York because it was free and he didn't have any money.

After graduating with an accounting degree and working for another accountant for 10 years, he started his own firm. The thing that I always remember, and had enormous influence on me, was that he loved what he did and he loved business. I can remember from the time I was a little girl sitting at the dinner table and listening to all the stories about my father's clients' businesses, about starting them up, and so on. He always spoke about them with enormous passion, and so I became aware of and interested in business when I was really pretty little.

When I was about ten I got wind of what the stock market was. It was around this time when my father bought me my first shares of stock. I remember it was ITT. Then every morning I'd look at the stock market pages. I've been looking at them ever since. I remember being in the seventh grade and writing an essay on the stock market, and the teacher was so taken by its sophistication that he had me read it in front of the whole class. In retrospect, I guess it was pretty unusual, given that in these times women were mostly only taking care of the house and children. The fact that my father would do that with his daughter was a pretty wonderful thing.

There was just a belief from the beginning that I could be and do whatever I wanted to do. The fact that I was female had nothing to do with anything. It was not necessarily a topic of conversation. It was more the absence of any obstacles. If I could dream about doing something, there was no reason I could not achieve it.

My father was so passionate and a bit of a contrarian. He enjoyed taking a contrary point of view, and while I'm not like that at all, I am never afraid to ask a question that might seem a little disruptive. I want to understand other points of view so I can find my own place in what I think about an issue.

I was sitting in a presentation once. I was the only woman and the only outsider, but I was there as a representative of my company. It was a presentation by one of the big consulting companies, and their recommendation was basically that my client abandon the business they were in and move to a related field. The thing that I found just incredible was that nobody around the table was questioning that recommendation. Now, sometimes, often times, companies have no intention of doing what consultants tell them to do, but I could not bear to just sit there without saying, "Wait a second. You mean we're getting out of the business you've been doing for decades and going in another direction? What about the brand and what about people's expectations and 100 years of history?" I'm perfectly comfortable playing that role and sometimes people in meetings will purposely use me that way. They know I'll ask the question that everybody is thinking about. I'm not afraid to ask the obvious hard question.

My father truly seized life. He wrung as much out of it as he possibly could. He was extremely spontaneous. If there were an opportunity to see something or do something, even if it meant you had to drive out of your way or wouldn't go to sleep on time and might be a little tired in the morning, he would seize it. That is a value set that I took from him.

When my oldest child was in the third grade, it was October and I got a call offering me some New York Yankees playoff tickets for a day game during the week. So that morning I pulled Teddy, my son, out of school. But first I had to lie – talk about a value set! I went to the school and told them we were having a bit of a family emergency. Of course, they were very solicitous and Teddy did not know what was happening because I was acting grave. So when I got in the car I told him, "There's no family problem. We're going to the Yankees game!"

He's 29 now, just married, and neither he nor I will ever forget it. That was very much like my father. He just would have seized the moment and gone to the game.

I've tried to practice that way of thinking all the way through, in everything I do.

JOHN J. LENNON

JOHN LENNON is CEO and Director of Pyramid Breweries, Inc. Prior to that position he was president and CEO of Beck's North America. He has served on the board of directors of several leading brewing and soft drink operations, including Jamaica's D&G (producer of Red Stripe beer), Grenada Brewery (where he was named Acting Chairman), St. Vincent Brewery and Windward and Leeward Brewery (a Heineken subsidiary, based in St. Lucia).

Lennon holds an MBA from Syracuse University and is married to Gail Workman. They have two children.

My father's life is typical of "the greatest generation." He was born in 1922 in New Rochelle, New York, to immigrant parents who had the courage and vision to want to bestow the promise of America upon their children and future generations.

He served in the Army during World War II. The day after Pearl Harbor was attacked, he went to enlist but, because of bad eyesight, he had to literally memorize the eye chart in order to pass the physical. He defended the nation from ruthless fascism in the war as one of Ike's citizen soldiers, and it proved to be the great and lasting adventure of his life. To this day he maintains deep and abiding friendships with his

Army buddies from the 386th who remain forever etched with youthful vigor and vitality.

He went to school at Northwestern University on the G.I. grant after the war and started his career at CBS Television after graduation. He did everything from operating a boom mike on the *Arthur Godfrey Show* to engineering and developing new cameras and equipment that were used for broadcast. We were the first people on our block to have a color TV.

My father had many mottoes that he lived by:

"Honor your commitments."

"Work hard. Hard work will provide rewards, even if it is just the satisfaction of knowing that you completed a job."

"Play hard. Enjoy your free time actively, not passively."

"Don't quit – be persistent."

"Maintain a sense of humor through it all."

But two things stand out as the greatest gifts and characteristics my father instilled in me, and they have everything to do with character and integrity.

No. 1 was that when we moved to a neighborhood that was very racially mixed in the early 1960s, my father taught us to treat everybody equally, no matter what their station in life. Have respect for all, no matter what race, creed, political point of view or social status. He totally bought into the American value of life, that everyone is created equal, and I've really tried to take that with me and pass it on.

No. 2 is the tremendous sense of loyalty that I take with me. The best embodiment of that was demonstrated when I was 14 (as the oldest of four kids) and my mother came down with multiple sclerosis. For a good part of her adult life thereafter she was deteriorating both physically and emotionally. It was very difficult for her to deal with. She lived for many years with the disease, but the emotional aspect of the illness made it, at times, difficult to live with her. She took out a lot of her frustration on my father, and being an Irish Catholic family, we did not go to see psychiatrists. My father was a beacon of stability that guided us through the turbulent seas of her struggle, and he always remained very, very loyal to her, took care of her and showed great respect to her right through the end. It was basically 20 years that were very difficult for him in the throes of uncertainty of that disease.

Her death was a liberating experience for him in many ways, but at the same time, for two decades of his life he still took very good care of her and looked after her. I learned a lot from his example. Many other guys would have run the other way.

Our family recently celebrated his 80th birthday and took stock of all the precious gifts he has bestowed upon us. I am deeply moved and profoundly grateful for all he has done for me, for in my eyes he is truly a hero.

REV. EDWARD A. MALLOY, C.S.C., PH.D.

The 16th president of the University of Notre Dame, **FATHER MALLOY** was elected by the Board of Trustees in 1986 after having served five years as vice president and associate provost. Father Malloy is a full professor in the Department of Theology and has been a member of the Notre Dame faculty since 1974.

Father Malloy earned his doctorate in Christian ethics from Vanderbilt University in 1975, and Vanderbilt honored him in 1998 with the establishment of a chair in Catholic studies in his name. He has received 12 honorary degrees.

He has written four books and has authored more than 50 articles and book chapters. An ethicist by training, he is a member of the Catholic Theological Society of America and the Society of Christian Ethics.

Father Malloy's service to higher education includes membership on the boards of Vanderbilt University and the Universities of Portland and St. Thomas.

A native of Washington, D.C., Father Malloy was born May 3, 1941.

Reverend Edward A. Malloy holds a Ph.D., is president of one of America's premier private universities, was a driving force in the 1997

President's Service Summit, serves as the chair or a board member for at least eight different institutions that support higher learning, has met Presidents, the Pope and Lou Holtz. So what do the students of Notre Dame call this esteemed man of letters and academia? Monk.

His father was a claims adjuster for the transit company in Scranton, Pennsylvania, when he was born. A high school graduate, he worked hard but always had time for his three children (Edward and two sisters).

"When my father was young, he lost a kidney from infection and was never an athlete, but I was," recalls Father Malloy. "So he made time for me to play catch or basketball. Where he was truly extraordinary was, as I got older, he was always there to drive me or my sisters to our activities. He spent all those discretionary moments taking us to Washington Senators games or encouraging or spending time with us on our homework." This desire to play an active and nurturing role was not lost on the son.

Father Malloy is truly at home in the academic world and has brought new beliefs and techniques to his role as president. He credits his father for this in many respects. "He didn't try to make me into something I wasn't. He simply tried to bring out the best in me."

He is one of only a handful of university presidents who still teach at their universities. He teaches a freshman class each fall semester that includes various novels and movies depicting a vast array of cultures and themes. He also lives in on-campus student housing, as opposed to a large home that is usually a perk for the administrative head of a university. Up until his 57th birthday, Father Malloy played basketball on a pick-up but fairly competitive basis with his students. He continued this until a shoulder injury made shooting too painful. "I figured why play basketball if you can't shoot? Then all you could do was pass and play defense," he recalls, tongue firmly placed in cheek. "The reason I live in a student dormitory and I teach, in addition to my presidential duties, is that I've found that it's a way of giving back." That's a habit taken from his father, who helped serve his church as a tour guide at the Shrine of the Immaculate Conception in Washington up until the day he died of a heart attack at the age of 77. "Because my undergraduate education was paid for by a basketball scholarship and my doctoral and seminary work was paid for by academic scholarship, it allows me to help students make the transition smoothly and give them the confidence they need to succeed at Notre Dame."

His father was a great believer in education, and Father Malloy took his convictions to heart. "He always believed in education as a route to maximizing your options. I remember saying to him one time when I was young that I hope to some day have a job like him. He told me, 'Under no circumstances do I want you to have a job like I had.' He said the reason that he was never promoted in his job was because of his level of education. He said his dream for me was to get all the education I was capable of and to have a lot of options. He told me he hated his job for a long time but he was happy to work so that I could have a lot more freedom in my work than he did."

As an educator, Father Malloy has worked to shape lives and build intelligent, moral men and women. He has done so unconventionally and has thrived in his endeavor. His relationship with his father was one of love and respect, and his father was able to see his dreams of education for his son fulfilled. "About a year before he died, I was on sabbatical and he was able to come visit me in Berkeley, California, for a week. We had an opportunity to spend a lot of concentrated time together, and I know that was comforting for him."

The boy whose father had wanted so much to give him an education has in turn chosen to dedicate his life to teaching thousands of young minds. He has taken a unique and successful approach to his duties and has strengthened Notre Dame on every level. He has taken his father's philosophy and amplified it.

COOPER, ELI & PEYTON MANNING

The three sons of professional and college football legend Archie Manning have all excelled in athletics, in the classroom and in life.

COOPER, the eldest, graduated from the University of Mississippi and is an institutional broker in New Orleans. As a freshman member of the Ole Miss football team in 1992, he had a promising career ended by a congenital narrowing of the spinal canal and a bulging disk in his neck. His athletic competitiveness has served him well in business, however. He is married and has two children.

PEYTON, the second born, has excelled since high school on the gridiron. After winning accolades as arguably the top prep quarterback in America, he attended and graduated from the University of Tennessee in three years. He returned for his senior year, brought the Volunteers back to national prominence and was runner-up for the Heisman Trophy, awarded annually to the country's top college football player. He has continued his success in the National Football League with the Indianapolis Colts, reaching the Pro-Bowl four times in his first six years and making the Colts perennial contenders. Peyton was married in 2001.

ELI, the youngest, has carried on the Manning tradition at the quarterback position. During his senior year in high school, he was named All-American. He chose to attend Ole Miss, like his father before him. At Ole Miss he won the Maxwell Award for the nation's top collegiate player, and the Johnny Unitas Golden Arm Award for the nation's top senior quarterback. He finished third in the 2003 Heisman Trophy balloting and was the top pick of The New York Giants in the 2004 NFL Draft.

We always knew our dad was a quarterback.

Football was a big part of our childhood, and that was kind of cool. Athletics as a whole were always there, and we were always involved in sports. We all wanted to be just like our dad, maybe even a little more so than other kids. I am not sure if it is the same if your dad is a lawyer or a doctor, but with us, even our friends looked up to him. That was particularly neat as a kid growing up in the neighborhood. Because of his hours, he always had time for us, so when we played football he would be permanent quarterback. Everyone was dying to play. We had a lot of games and a lot of memories in the yard with our friends and Dad.

Early in life when we chose to participate in activities, he encouraged us. We adored sports, so they were natural fits. As we got older, he used to tell us that if we wanted to play the guitar or be on the chess team, there were only a couple of rules:

- If we started, we were not allowed to quit.

- If we had ambitions to take it to the next level, he would help us figure out what it takes to do so, but we could not count on him to hold our hand or push us to do it.

Our dad is a tad bashful, very competitive, has an element of seriousness, and is definitely the disciplinarian out of our two parents. He has instilled certain characteristics in all of us. Peyton is the most like our father. He is all business and driven. He took what Dad has and moved it to another level. Eli, on the other hand, is the most quiet and reserved of the three of us. You are not going to hear him yell, hoot and holler. He does not want the attention on himself all the time. He feels that blending in is just as comfortable as taking the lead and, in essence, leading by example. Conversely, no one is quite sure where Cooper came from. Maybe he got a little of our father's speed on the football field. Personality wise, he tried to be like him as much as he could, on the humble side, but we are not sure it ever quite stuck. Our mom is a little bit more outgoing, a little more fun loving, and Cooper's enjoyment of a good time may have come from her.

We were always in awe of Dad's patience. Being in the limelight as he has always been, people were tugging on him to sign this, that and the other thing. Whether it was natural or just important to Dad, he always wanted to act respectfully, kindly, and make everyone feel good. Even when he was at dinner with our family and some knucklehead came up to the table wanting to take a picture, he responded with grace, and that carried through to us in a big way. At the same time, because we were a little more in the public eye, he made it clear that whether you like it or not, people are going to know who you are, are going to want to talk about you and, most importantly, are going to be critical. So, he told us, life may not be fair in that respect, and we have to keep our noses clean. If we screwed up a little bit, it would get blown out of proportion and could turn awful. His advice was to make sure to associate with the right folks and not get into too much trouble. Sometimes it was easier said than done.

When we were growing up, Dad went to all our games. He made a big effort to be there and be supportive, but he was always very quiet. There were very loud parents in the stands, but Dad was notorious for standing at the top of the bleachers with his mouth tightly closed. Later, this was even more the case when there was a chance he could be on camera. He wanted to do his best to remain as stoic as possible. Obviously, there was some celebrating for touchdowns, but he kept his expression to a very bare minimum following an interception. He usually wore his hat and his headphones to listen to the broadcast of the game. He is very incognito and not necessarily a delight to sit next to, because he cannot hear what you are saying. It is a bit like sitting next to nobody.

One thing that would anger Dad, especially with Cooper and Peyton, who were two years apart, was our fighting. He was always envious of having a brother. Many times he told us how lucky we were to have each other. Of course, at the time we did not feel lucky; we just knew that whoever won in basketball might get a bloody nose. We were brothers and competitive and just fought. Because dad had a sister, he tried to teach us how fortunate we were to have one another, and he tried to make us more pals than rivals at each other's throats.

We went to services every Sunday morning at the Baptist church when we were growing up. We had to be brought kicking and screaming. We hated it. But Mom and Dad made us go, and every Sunday morning there was a tussle. We had to get up early and get dressed up. There was nothing worse than putting on dress-up clothes on a day off, when you could be out running and playing. That was always a constant battle, but attending church was an important part of our youth.

With our education Dad was not so tough on grades as he was on effort. If a teacher thought we were working hard and were putting in the hours but still got a "C" or a "B", he was all right with it. But if we were not working hard, we would have a problem with him – or, more rightly, he would have a problem with us – no matter what our grade.

Cooper has two young children, and Dad and Mom have adored and embraced the idea of being grandparents. It has been a great luxury having them living in New Orleans, the same town where Cooper resides. There is a sense, in Cooper's mind, of trying to live up to how we grew up – to provide his children with the same kind of childhood we had. We honestly do not have one single complaint with the way we were raised. If anything, we might just have a hard time measuring up. There is always a sense of needing to do more – sort of an automatic guilt. In a way, at the risk of sounding cocky, we hope our kids can grow up the way we did, because everyone turned out pretty well.

There was a time 20 years ago when someone interviewed Dad about being honored as a "Legend of Mississippi." The interviewer asked him how he would like to be remembered, and he said very simply, "As a good guy." That has always stuck with us. We have always tried to be that way to emulate him. We want people to describe us that way, whether it is a friend, a parking attendant, a waiter or anybody. It behoves you in the long run to treat everyone with respect. We may not have done as good a job as he has, but we have tried to put forth the effort with him in mind.

JOHN K. MARA

JOHN K. MARA, the oldest son of New York Giants President Wellington Mara, begins his thirteenth season with the Giants as Executive Vice President and General Counsel. In his present position, Mara, who joined the Giants in 1991, is responsible for all administrative, legal and financial aspects of the organization and reports directly to the Co-Chief Executive Officers, Wellington Mara and Preston Robert Tisch.

Mara also serves on the influential NFL Competition Committee, which studies all aspects of the game and recommends rules and policy changes to NFL clubs, and the NFL Employee Benefits Committee.

Mara was born in New York City on December 1, 1954, grew up in Westchester County in White Plains, and graduated from Iona Prep High School in New Rochelle. He attended Boston College, where he received a B.S. degree in marketing, graduating with *cum laude* honors in 1976. Mara earned his law degree from Fordham University in 1979. Mara serves on the Board of Directors of Saint Vincent's Hospital in Harrison, New York, The School of the Holy Child, also in Harrison, Iona Preparatory School in New Rochelle, and Catholic Community Services of Newark, New Jersey.

John and his wife, the former Denise Walter, are the parents of five children: Lauren, 22; Courtney, 20; John Jr., 19; Christine, 17; and Erin, 13. The Mara family resides in Harrison.

Many of my earliest memories with my father center around his taking my brothers and me to Yankee Stadium, not only for our Giants home games but also for the Saturday morning practice before a game. He allowed us to run around on the field and wander in the locker room, which we shared with the Yankees at the time.

One of the things that sticks with me to this day is how strict and stringent he was when it came to our religious beliefs. There was never, ever any excuse to miss Catholic mass on Sunday or any other Holy Day of Obligation. You could be on your deathbed but you were expected to be at mass on Sunday mornings. My kids would probably say I am just as strict, maybe one of the toughest dads on Earth, but I do not think I am quite as strict as my father was. In either case, it is definitely something I have tried to pass on to my own children.

There is one story in particular that really illustrates my father's faith and desire for me to follow in his footsteps. It took place not too long ago. I was a grown man with children, practicing law in Manhattan and in the middle of a very big trial. He always had a habit (which he does to this very day) of reminding us about Holy Days. So there I was in the middle of a big case, preparing for the next day's testimony, my fifth child just about to be born, and he called the office around 7:00 and asked if I had gone to mass that day. I told him I had not. He proceeded to berate me for the next 10 minutes, saying I had lost my values, and could I not have sacrificed 15 minutes of sleep in the morning and gone to mass? It was really one of the most unpleasant conversations I have ever had with him, and he hung up the phone on me.

I felt absolutely miserable.

About 10 minutes later he called back to tell me that he was sorry he was so tough on me, that he loved me and that he had a lot of respect for me, was proud of me and did not mean to sound the way he did.

He practically reduced me to tears, but just as he was about to hang up he said, "And by the way, I checked and there is a church over on

43rd Street called St. Agnes, and they have an 8:00 p.m. mass this evening. You can make it if you hurry."

And I went.

He would always take my brothers and me to Yankee Stadium every year for Bat Day. It was something we looked forward to, not only to go to the game but to get a free baseball bat.

One particular year, when I was ten or eleven, we were coming out of the stadium, and I had one of the bats with a Mickey Mantle signature engraved on the barrel. I was so happy with it. As we were walking to our car, a kid about my age, in a neighborhood right by the stadium, started walking along with us and asking questions about the game, and where did we get those bats?

My father pulled me aside and said, "Why don't you give that bat to this boy?" And I said, "What? Are you kidding? It's got Mickey Mantle on it." And he replied, "How many of those bats do you have at home?" I probably had four or five, but before I could answer my dad said, "This kid probably doesn't have any. It will mean a lot more to him than it will ever mean to you."

So, very reluctantly, I gave him the bat. At first he refused to take it – he thought there was a catch and was not sure whether to trust us – but eventually he took it. To this day I will never forget the expression on his face, and I remember my father sitting me down that night and explaining that the joy and pleasure you get in giving is much greater than what you get from receiving and accumulating material things. It is something that stuck with me to this day – a lesson I will never forget.

If there is one characteristic that people use to describe my father, and hopefully myself, it is loyalty. Loyalty to old friends, to former players and to the team's fans has always been so important to my father. I cannot tell you how many old friends and players he has helped either financially or in numerous other ways, whether it be getting them proper medical attention or going to visit them in the hospital.

For years the joke around the Giants used to be that nobody who worked there ever exited on their feet, they usually were carried out on a stretcher after they died. We just did not fire people. I think that is still the case (with the exception of the occasional manager) and a characteristic of us today. I think it goes back to the one lesson my father tried to teach us over and over again. He wanted us, above all else, to treat people the same way you want them to treat you. He really drummed it into our heads. The Golden Rule was something he preached and he lives.

It is a pretty good way to live your life, and I try to emulate it every day.

MARY MATALIN

MARY MATALIN formerly served as assistant to President George W. Bush and counselor to Vice President Cheney and was the first White House official to hold a double title.

Matalin has made frequent television appearances as a political commentator and has written for various periodicals, including *Newsweek* and the *Los Angeles Times.* Matalin also co-authored the best-selling political campaign book *All's Fair: Love, War and Running for President* with her husband, James Carville, who was the chief campaign strategist for Clinton/Gore in 1992.

Her eclectic political career has seen her host television programs, star in the critically acclaimed HBO docudrama *K Street* and even play the role of corporate pitch-woman. She is a favorite of the news-related talk shows, where she appears on a frequent basis.

She lives in Virginia with her husband and two daughters.

Growing up, I remember my father holding my hand and taking me to the store, to the park, everywhere. I was always in tow. I remember always having a little hand in his big hand. It is a wonderful memory. He is a conservative, not just politically, but truly a conservative. He has very well formed, articulate opinions on everything. He reads everything, thinks about everything he reads, and really utilizes the education he gave himself through the GI Bill. He is a political junkie, and when we talk it is one of my great joys in life. We talk endlessly regarding the day's events – he follows it all. We did not grow up sharing politics, but we are both kind of obsessed with it now. He gives me a lot more scoops than you would think, because I do not always have as much time as I need to stay informed. He's like my one-man focus group.

He was always working. This is a guy who worked the swing shift in the steel mill, received a degree in mechanical engineering and then went on and earned an MBA from Purdue. He is a hard-working man who set an incredibly great example.

I see my father in me as a much weaker, diluted version. He was the extreme version of perseverance, tenacity, honesty and ethics. I'm not saying that I'm dishonest or unethical, just that he was acutely so. He does not understand spin in politics. He does not see how I can withstand false attacks and negative, untruthful things like that. He is the son of eastern European immigrants and did not speak English until he was forced to when he went to school. To his dying day, my grandfather's English was almost indecipherable, but he had a real sense of that American work ethic that was peculiar to the immigrants and that really made this country grow. Honesty and integrity were large parts of that.

My father has a huge sense of patriotism and reverence for freedom, which I do have in mass quantities and I know that I got that from him. One thing he has that I wish I did is that he's a very logical, methodical thinker, and I'm more of a straight-from-the-hip person.

All the good stuff I have, I got from him, and all the bad stuff I just sort of made up.

He wanted us to think we could do anything. He was ahead of his time to instill that kind of confidence and optimism in his girls. Parents back then, particularly in a blue-collar area like ours, did not even encourage girls to go to college. He used to sit me down all the time and say, "You can do anything."

We would also see by watching him. He picked up – much older than people should – things like skiing, sailing and all these other man-versus-weather hobbies. He learned guitar out of nowhere, not that he was any good, but my mother learned the bass and I always played the accordion (which is a very weird instrument that grandchildren of immigrants are forced to learn), and my sister and brother also played. He was at all times pushing the envelope beyond and always stretching himself.

He's a risk taker. I think what we learned from that is to reach out and not be afraid to fail. I do not think he ever failed at anything, but we had the sense that if you tried, that was the equivalent of succeeding – and he told us that all the time.

He is very competitive, and being able to compete is a good thing he instilled in us. One time while racing a sailboat, my sister and I were crewing for him and my hiking straps (which held me in the boat) broke when we were tacking and the boat was on its side. I fell backwards into the water, and he left me there until my sister reminded him that any boat with someone overboard was automatically disqualified. Otherwise, he would have never come back to get me during the race. I totally understood and was not even remotely mad. I was upset that he came back to get me. It sounds cold in the retelling of it, but it was not. It was a great life lesson.

As a parent, the way I live is not far from the way he lived, probably because kids learn by example. The research bears this out. There is so much pressure everywhere else in a child's world, but I think James and I, at this stage in our lives, have better judgment, greater wisdom, more patience, with a kind of a stubborn world view. We are in the position to be able to do a lot of things with our kids that my parents could not do. But the thing that was instilled in me is the gratefulness for what you have, and humility.

He pushed us by example, but he never pressured us or made us feel guilty. You just wanted to live up to his example, and that is still so. The guy is 74 years old, he has incurable cancer, he's in remission and he is working a 40-hour week at the election commission, checking voting machines and in charge of recounts. He is an amazing man. He still goes out dancing, plays golf and always does physical exercise. He's just a man who has lived large and – as all research shows, and with me as an expert witness – he is a living example of the incredible influence fathers have on their daughters.

KENNY MAYNE III

KENNY MAYNE – known for his offbeat style, dry humor, unique sayings ("Thanks for having electricity.") and home-run calls *("I am amused by the simplicity of this game!")* – has served in a variety of roles in nearly 10 years with ESPN, the sports network.

Prior to joining ESPN, Mayne was a freelance reporter and field producer for the network from 1990-1994. "During that time," Mayne says, "I pursued only one full-time television job – ESPN. I had the ESPN 800-number and called all the time with story ideas. I guess they finally decided it was less expensive to hire me than to keep paying for my phone calls."

A native of Kent, Washington, Mayne was born September 1, 1959. He attended Wenatchee Valley Community College, where he was an honorable mention junior college All-America quarterback in 1978. He graduated from the University of Nevada-Las Vegas in 1982 with a Bachelor of Arts degree in broadcasting. While at UNLV, Mayne played football for two years and later signed as a free agent with the Seattle Seahawks (1982). Mayne is married and resides in Connecticut.

Kenny Mayne has lived a life full of tremendous highs and devastating lows. He has held blue-collar jobs and been a cult hero to millions of sports fans through his work on television. He has a wonderful wife and two daughters and yet has lost two children, one stillborn and one a few months after his birth. Through it all, he has felt his father's impact on his life through humor, a positive outlook on humanity and the ability to see the future as a very positive place.

"My father, Kenneth Wheelock Mayne, Jr., was born in Iowa in the mid-1920s. He died a few days before our daughter was born. He worked for United Airlines and was a very hard worker. He always applied for extra overtime because it was important that the family be taken care of."

Did the son receive any of his trademark quirky comic personality from his father? "I received some of my humorous characteristics from him. He wasn't necessarily the funniest guy in the room, but he was known for his dry, quick wit. He reminded me of a cross between Dick Van Dyke and Johnny Carson.

"The thing that struck me most about him was that he was such a humble person and always pushed for inclusion. He used to tell my sisters that if they were going to have a party, they should invite everyone or no one. He didn't want anybody left out who was considered less popular. When we had a memorial service for him, everyone who spoke said how welcomed they always felt, how we always had our doors open, that our home was a place where friends could stay if they had trouble with their families. He was always very welcoming.

"He wanted us to always open our hearts to the little guys. That's helped me and my wife make a commitment to help people who are a little less fortunate. It just feels right to do that. I see my father in myself when it comes to trying to help others.

"A few years ago, there was a *New York Times* article about a family living about an hour south of Chicago that was in extremely poor conditions, really poverty stricken. So my wife and I contacted the writer of the story and arranged to help the family. We supported them for a year to get them on their feet. That's something my dad would have done."

Sometimes being a highly recognizable television personality can create ego problems for individuals, but the humility that Kenny's father instilled in him keeps him modest. "When I'm at home taking out the garbage or helping out with my two daughters, Riley and Anna, I'm so far removed from everything at ESPN. So when I go out into the field on assignment to do a story, it tends to keep me grounded."

Kenny was always taught to do a good job and encouraged at every turn by his dad. "He was always proud of us, whether it was a small thing or something truly significant. I remember I was going through a pretty rough time in my life in the early '90s. I'd left a TV job in Seattle for no great reason, and I was doing a bunch of 'pay the bills' jobs. I was assembling garbage cans and working for a telemarketing company. But he was so proud of me when I had a great day at the telemarketing job. He was just looking for anything to give me a little more hope. It wasn't about the money. We didn't grow up rich by any means, but we always felt secure that tomorrow would be a better day."

That philosophy has helped Kenny through some of the toughest days a father can endure. In 1996 Kenny and his wife Laura became pregnant with twins, only to deliver the babies three months premature. One of the children, Creighton, was stillborn; the other, Connor, was born weighing less than two pounds. After six months and numerous operations, Connor passed away one day after taking Laura's breast milk for the first time. "We never knew how my father would cope with it," Kenny says, referring to the tragic events, "if he would have the right thing to say. He wasn't real outgoing with his feelings, and that made it difficult for him to deal with it. But when Connor lived for six months and he came to visit him a few times, I saw something in him that I hadn't seen before. He had a braver heart and a deeper passion than I'd realized before."

For those who know Kenny Mayne III as a friend, a husband and a father, it is apparent that those characteristics have been passed on.

MICHAEL REAGAN

MICHAEL REAGAN, the eldest son of former President Ronald Reagan, is heard daily by more than five million listeners via his nationally syndicated talk radio program, "the very independent Michael Reagan Show." The show airs on more than 200 stations in the U.S. and for the world at reaganradio.com.

Reagan's radio career began with an appearance as a guest host on Michael Jackson's program from KABC in Los Angeles. He was then host of a top-rated local radio program on San Diego's KSDO before launching his national program in 1992, where he has earned record ratings as the No. 1 host in dozens of markets.

Prior to launching the national program, Reagan set world records in powerboat racing. His racing raised more than $1.5 million for charities like the Cystic Fibrosis and Diabetes Foundations and the Statue of Liberty Restoration Fund. His efforts were recognized when he became a recipient of the "Victor Award" for outstanding sports and humanitarian achievement.

Reagan also serves on the board for the John Douglas French Alzheimer's Association and has authored many successful books, including his best-selling autobiography, *On the Outside Looking In,* and *The Common Sense of An Uncommon Man: The Wit, Wisdom and Eternal Optimism of Ronald Reagan.* He and his wife, Colleen, have two children and reside in Sherman Oaks, California.

My earliest recollections of my dad are of his teaching me how to swim, like he taught all of us Reagans, when I was just a child. I remember his picking me up on Saturdays, because my parents divorced when I was three. He would either come to my school (when I reached that age), or he would come get me at home. We always went up to Rancho del Cielo, his "Ranch in the Sky." He once described it by saying, "From the first day we saw it, Rancho del Cielo cast a spell over us. No place before or since has ever given me the joy and serenity it does."

He would take me horseback riding, swimming, what have you, and they were wonderful times. Saturdays were always spent on the range, and often times Sundays would be spent going to church with his mother, Nellie. He spent weekends with both my sister Maureen and me, bringing us to the country, and those are the times I really looked forward to. I would just sit on the curb and wait for his car to come around Sunset Boulevard, turn down Beverly Glenn and come pick me up so the fun could begin.

My dad was not a really big star during my youth; my mother, Jane Wyman, was. All I knew was I lived in really nice, big houses and had maids and cooks and people waiting on us all the time. But the reality is that it was tough. With most children, it is usually all about them. They feel, and many times are treated, like the only thing on the planet. It's I, I, I. It was difficult because kids want to be in the spotlight, but in Hollywood it is the parents who are often in the spotlight. Everybody is fighting for the glow. The good side was that I had parents who loved me; the bad side was in that industry there were many times they were not home because of location shoots and the like. Subsequently, we and many kids of our era were sent off to boarding school, so we did not really get to grow up with our parents or have the relationships with them that other kids had. My dad tried to make up for that when we would come home on weekends.

Dad was one of those people who – as Maureen and I used to joke – when asked what time it was would tell you how the watch was made. You did not ask him too many questions. One time when I was eight years old, I asked him for a larger allowance and got an economics lesson. I got a tutorial on how much he paid in taxes, the percentage he retained after taxes, and then he promised me that when the American people elected a President who gave him a tax cut he would give me a larger percentage of his income. So I found myself at the age of eight rooting for a fiscal conservative to attain the Presidency. All I did was ask for another dollar.

He taught by doing. To teach me patience, he would not tell me to be patient. Rather we would go hunting in the afternoon with a single-action .22 caliber rifle when I was nine years old. After horseback riding in the morning, we would go looking for ground squirrels. We would sit stone still waiting for one of those critters to pop its head up. I would be running all over the place shooting at anything that moved, and he would sit me down and have me focus on the task. Not that it worked, but he tried. But there was a reason for the hunting beyond just for sport. It was because those squirrels would dig holes, and he had horses that he did not want stepping into those holes, breaking a leg and having to be put down. So it was a duty. If you are going to ride a horse, then you need to look after the horse. You have to put it away, not wet but dry. He would teach me with his actions and reinforce it with our own.

An ideal that was so apparent in his character, his presidency and that he passed on to me was that when you take a stand, you should know why you take it. He knew why he took positions, but I had to learn that. One of the reasons he did this so well is because he understood himself better than anybody. I learned that too and have realized what I am, in order to accomplish the things that I want to do in life.

Dad really showed me how important family is. It is of the utmost importance. The No. 1 thing he taught me was to stay married and how important it is to be true to that woman. It is wonderful to know that when you come home every night there is a woman on the other side of that door who really loves you. Treat her with respect.

I really did not get political until the late 1970s. When I was out campaigning for him, it almost happened by osmosis and the political side kicked in. That was another way in which Dad and I were able to bond. He and I, as much as anybody else in the family, agreed politically. In fact, I agreed with him *more* than anybody else in the family.

The other bond that we share is that we are both Christians. That was ultimately the strongest similarity that kept our bond strong. To this day we share the Christian faith that we both have.

I do pray, as my father always has, and I have a lot of people who pray for me, as does my father. I am the man I am because others, like my wife, have always prayed for me. Dad prayed to God and offered up his presidency to God, and I think that was good for the country. It was wonderful that my dad and I were able to talk about God and talk about Christ and share our faith with each other. We went from a father picking up his young eight-year-old son on Beverly Glenn to go horseback riding and learning life's lessons, to a deep spiritual sharing we had as men.

There are some differences between me and my father as a parent. That's because of the nature of the beast. My dad was in the position where he had two children from his first marriage to my mother and two children from his second to Nancy. He had to do the mighty dance, which is not easy when you have four kids hitting on you from all angles, and there were some jealousy issues. He was able to do it well, and boy, was he an easy touch. It was the mothers who were the tough ones in the family. He was a pussy cat. I always went to him to get everything.

He never punished us. Dad would just look at you. He always made you feel guilty about doing something wrong. The mothers would punish you, so it was definitely better to be with Dad. But you did not want to disappoint Ronald Reagan.

I loved to ride horses and always wanted my own. When I was ten he came to me and said, "Michael, I do not want you to feel bad, but there's a man I know who has a son about your age and he is going to get his boy a horse for Christmas. But they have no place to keep the horse until then, and I am allowing them to keep it here. Also, the horse needs to be rideable for the boy, so I am asking you, when you come up to the ranch, to help work out the horse in the ring and get it used to a child your size and age. That way when the boy gets the horse for Christmas, it will be used to the weight and demeanor."

I replied to my dad with tears in my eyes and a quivering voice,

"Yes, Dad, sure I'll do it."

And at the same time I was thinking about kicking him in the shins for even mentioning another boy my age who was getting his own horse! What about me?

So every Saturday for more than two months I went out to the ranch, got the horse (whom I had named Rebel) out of the stall, put the tether on it and took him to the ring, where dad would be in the center. We would then go in circles with me on the horse for about half an hour.

I fell in love with this horse.

Finally Christmas was just a couple of days away, and Dad called me on the phone at the house and told me the boy's father was coming the next day to get the horse because he now had a stable for him. He asked me if I wanted to ride with him to meet the man and his boy and, most importantly, to say goodbye to Rebel. And again, with tears streaming down my face, I said, "Yes, I'll go."

So dad picked me up at home and took me out to the ranch and said, "Why don't you go out and get Rebel and we'll get everything ready inside."

I went out to the barn and to Rebel's stall with watery eyes, undid the latch, opened the door and inside there was Rebel, a beautiful Palomino, looking at me – freshly washed and newly cleaned with a golden mane and a big red ribbon around the neck with a card on it that said, "To Michael, Merry Christmas, Love Dad."

That was Dad. He wanted me to appreciate things and to work for them. That was the way he would come at you. He tried to make me feel like I had earned it.

And I did.

Sadly, Michael's father, Ronald Reagan, the fortieth President of The United States, died on June 5, 2004.

CAL RIPKEN, JR.

CAL RIPKEN is baseball's all-time Iron Man. He retired from baseball in October 2001, after 21 seasons with the Baltimore Orioles. His name appears in the record books repeatedly, most notably as one of only seven players in history to achieve 400 home runs and 3,000 hits. In 1995, Ripken broke Lou Gehrig's record for consecutive games played (2,130) and ended his own streak in 1998 after playing in 2,632 consecutive games. Although he finished his career at third base, this future Hall of Famer is still best known for redefining the position of shortstop.

Other on-field accolades include AL Rookie of the Year ('82), two-time AL Most Valuable Player ('83, '91), two-time Gold Glove recipient ('91, '92), two-time All-Star MVP ('91, '01) and 19 All-Star Game selections.

Years of charitable association with Baltimore Reads, the Ripken Learning Centers, and the Reading, Runs and Ripken program have helped promote adult and family literacy. The Kelly G. Ripken Program at Johns Hopkins Hospital assists with thyroid education and patient care. In honor of his record-breaking feat in 1995, the Cal Ripken Jr./Lou Gehrig ALS Research Fund was established to help find a cure for amyotrophic lateral sclerosis, or "Lou Gehrig's Disease."

Ripken resides in Maryland with his wife, Kelly, and their children, Rachel and Ryan.

Dad always applied lessons learned in baseball to life. He used to say that baseball emulates life, and even now I seem to do that in all my ventures away from baseball. I find that when I relate a problem to a similar situation in baseball, it's easier to solve.

For example, take communication in an office. In any environment there are different types of people, and how you get your message across can depend on the sensitivities of individuals. The same is true in baseball. There were certain players I played with whom I couldn't speak directly to. If I did, they would back away and feel like they were being criticized. So there was a certain way I had to present my message so it wouldn't ruffle feathers. To set your message apart and to be a good teacher, you have to understand who you are talking to and how they receive information. You phrase things differently; you may need to say the same thing in many different ways to drive the message home.

One of the things my dad taught me was to "celebrate the individual." What he meant is that each of us is unique, and we all have different talents and abilities that we should celebrate. There is no one way to do things and no one way to say things.

He also trained us to do things the right way, always. Never take the shortcut. Today I often look at my work and know that dad would be particularly proud of the way I did a job, by doing it right. It can apply to baseball or any other pursuit, even a task as small as shoveling snow or doing yard work.

As a father, I know I got my sense of responsibility from him. Dad taught me that words are not necessarily the most powerful thing – it's your actions that count most. We all make mistakes, and sometimes we don't do the right thing, but it is the consistency of your message coupled with your actions that builds credibility. I learned from my father that family is important and that you have a responsibility to your wife and children. There are going to be problems, life is going to be hard, there are going to be issues and differences of opinion, but you always come back to the closeness of your family to help solve and resolve things.

Dad was very neighborly, and I have fond memories of things he used to do to help other families in the neighborhood. If it snowed and people needed their sidewalks shoveled or to be dug out, Dad seemed to go overboard. He had some small plows and access to a farm tractor, and he would clear alleys and roads to make them safer. He did that because he knew he would be away a lot, and he wanted people to reciprocate and take care of his family, in certain ways, when he was not there. It all went back to the responsibility he felt for us.

As you grow up, you sometimes think your parents do not know what you're going through, but later on you find out they really did. For the most part you take their guidance, but there's a curiosity where you need to experience things on your own. As a parent, you hope your children's curiosity doesn't put them in danger. But when I would make a mistake or do something wrong, dad was always good about reacting in a way that would scare me, especially if it was a safety issue, for my own sake. He would raise the level of the importance so I would know when it was really, really bad.

One of my biggest life lessons came once when I stayed out late. I could not tell my friends that I had to be home earlier than they did, so I broke curfew and came back really late. Mom was worried and it made for a tough few hours for her, not knowing where I was. The next morning dad came to my room and said, "I need some help this morning."

"Help" meant he would take me out to the garden where we would weed or take rocks out, or do something physical where we worked close together. He didn't say anything for a while, but then he opened the conversation by saying, "Got in a little late last night."

He started talking through it, making me realize the ramifications of my actions. "You know, mom was really worried about you. A lot of things went through her head when you didn't call." He was very calm and patient, and it taught me a lesson.

The lesson is that in the heat of a moment, there are two ways you can handle things. In my case, he could have waited up until I got in at

2:00 a.m. and then gone at it right then when we were both on edge. Or, as he did, he could let everyone go to bed, reflect on the situation, and then, one on one, he could explain and really teach me something.

In baseball, people often make mistakes – a base running error or missing a sign – and the tendency for most people is to try and teach at that moment. They want to say, "What are you doing?" as the player walks off the field. Dad's approach was different. He would make a note of it, and then after the game or the next day he would talk to the person. His theory was that no one could really learn at the moment because you are so worried about playing the game, and you are embarrassed about the mistake. It would go something like this: "You made a bad base running mistake. You made the last out going to third when we were down 4 – 1. We can't take a chance in that situation because there is no real advantage in getting to third base. You know what though? You have really been running the bases aggressively, and I like that. So, nice job being aggressive, but I want you to realize there are times we can take a risk and there are times when we cannot."

It was that common sense and subtle brilliance that helped make my dad – and I hope myself – a very good coach, teacher, husband and father.

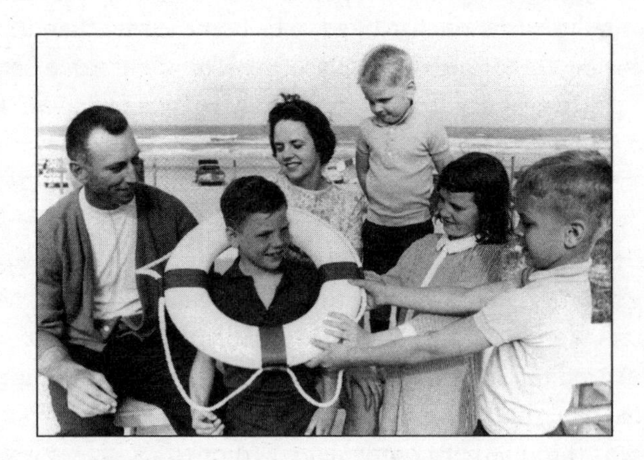

NOLAN RYAN

LYNN NOLAN RYAN, JR. was born on January 31, 1947, in Refugio, Texas. In 1965, after graduating from Alvin High School, Ryan signed a professional baseball contract with the New York Mets. His Major League debut with the Mets came in 1968. During a career that spanned 27 years, he played for four big league teams – the Mets, California Angels, Houston Astros and Texas Rangers. In that time, spanning four decades, Ryan set or eclipsed 51 major league pitching records, including seven no-hitters and 5,714 career strikeouts.

Ryan has the unique distinction of being the only player in Major League history to have his uniform number retired by three different teams – the Angels, Astros and Rangers. On January 5, 1999, the Baseball Writers Association of America awarded Ryan the ultimate recognition when he was elected to the National Baseball Hall of Fame in his first year of eligibility, by 98.79 percent of the vote, second highest of all time. Also in 1999, baseball fans across America voted him to the All-Century Team.

Ryan is the majority owner and Chairman of the board of The Express Bank in Alvin and Danbury, Texas, and owns Nolan Ryan's Waterfront Restaurant and Bass Inn near Three Rivers, Texas. He also owns and operates several cattle ranches in South Texas and a Class AA professional baseball franchise.

Ryan has given much back to the local community by serving on the boards of directors of the Nolan Ryan Foundation, the Justin Cowboy Crisis Fund, the Texas Water Foundation, the Natural Resources Foundation of Texas and the Alvin Community College Baseball Scholarship Fund.

He lives in Alvin, Texas, where he grew up, with his wife of 35 years, Ruth, also a native of Alvin. They have two sons and three grandchildren.

My dad was always home, and since we never traveled he was the constant in my life. Growing up, he and my mother were the focal point of our family. I worked with him at a very early age. That was important because I have four sisters, and in order for them to go to college, my dad and I became distributors of the *Houston Post* newspaper to earn extra money. It was a second job for him – during the day he was a supervisor for Pan American Petroleum Company. So from the time I was in second grade on, my father, my brother and I had a little family operation between one and four in the morning. When we delivered the paper, that was a customer service type of business, and dad's dedication to making sure our people were happy was always prevalent. We made sure that if there was a problem, it was taken care of properly. So I think that was a big influence on me and the way I approach things as an adult in my present business dealings.

I was the last of six kids. My dad came through the Depression with a big family too, and he always worked. There was very little time for sports. He had to have a job to afford a better opportunity for the rest of the family. Because of that, he did not have time to play anything. Even after becoming an adult, he did not take up golf or any of that stuff. There was no discretionary income or time. However, he was very supportive of us wanting to play sports.

I see a lot of the principles that were instilled in me by my dad in the way I have raised my own children. Of course, with each generation there are new challenges and different sets of circumstances, but the basic rules are the same. We were raised in the Baptist Church in

Alvin, Texas. In small towns, your church is a big part of the community environment and your upbringing, and our town was no exception. When I was playing in the Major Leagues, our lifestyle kept us on the road and we lived on a different schedule during the course of the season. During the off-season, I tried to spend as much time as possible with the family. When the kids were in school, Ruth and I would not travel unless we absolutely had to. We did not want to leave the kids. We wanted to have a normal life. It was especially good while I was playing in Houston for nine years. It allowed me to be with them as much as possible. I'm very thankful for that.

My benchmark for raising my kids was the same one my father had for me, and that is to allow them to pursue whatever interests they have, whether it is in sports or outside of sports. The main goal is for them to be happy and be fulfilled. We are very supportive, as was my dad, in whatever their interests are. I get a lot of satisfaction out of the fact that my sons have a passion for baseball, and we work together on the minor league level with the ball club that we own. That has been very gratifying.

As I look back on the influence my dad had in my life, both during and after baseball, it may have been his work ethic that had the biggest impact. Also, he told me many times that if you are going to do something, do it right. There are no shortcuts. I have a very early recollection of this philosophy. Every summer one of my jobs, besides mowing our yard and keeping it up, was painting the house. Dad would come home every afternoon and inspect what I had done that day. He taught me and educated me to do things properly. We had to chip the old paint off the house to start with. The paint in those days wouldn't peel off, so you had to chip it off, prepare what was underneath and then repaint it. This was not the kind of work you wanted to be doing as a kid, but it taught me to do things the right way the first time. It was my summer project every year, it had to be done properly, and he told me how I was doing every day when he got home, and that made a big impression on me.

Prior to signing with the New York Mets at 18 and leaving for the city, I had been out of the state of Texas only twice. Both times were for family vacations. One was to go to Ohio to visit my mother's mother, and the other time was to go to California to see one of my sisters who was living out there. New York was very much a culture shock for me, but dad did not necessarily offer any advice. He had faith that he had raised me well, the best he could do, and therefore had confidence in me as a person. Additionally, he was not any more familiar with what I was getting into than I was. He was never worried about me with regards to the trappings of fame and fortune because of our upbringing and the world we were raised in.

I am so happy that my father and mother had the opportunity to come up to New York to see us win the World Series when I was with the Mets in 1969. That was probably the highlight of my baseball career during his lifetime. I can also remember him driving me to the bus station in Houston when I was going into the Army. And that was probably one of the lowest points of my life. He was there to share both the good and the bad with me. He passed away early in my career, so he was not here to witness a lot of the things that happened to me in baseball, but he built the foundation that helped me become the man I am today. I feel very fortunate and blessed to have had my upbringing, because it was a very stable situation, a very good foundation, and it gave me the principles I apply to both my working and family environment today.

STEVE SABOL

As president of NFL Films, the most honored filmmaker in sports, **STEVE SABOL** is the artistic vision behind the studio that revolutionized the way America watches football.

Building on the entrepreneurial spirit of his father and founder of NFL Films, Sabol was named the 2002 Sports Executive of the Year by *Sporting News* magazine. Recently Sabol was honored with the prestigious Pete Rozelle Award, which is presented each year to a person who has made an outstanding contribution to the National Football League and to professional football. The innovative filmmaker joins a select group of honorees, including Vince Lombardi, Dan Rooney, Lamar Hunt, Tom Landry, Don Shula and Tex Schramm.

While NFL Films has won 84 Emmys, Sabol himself has received 28 of those for writing, cinematography, editing, directing and producing. No one in all of television has earned as many Emmys in as many different categories. He is one of a handful of people in the world to have attended every Super Bowl.

Sabol began his career in 1964 as a cinematographer working for his father at NFL Films. As an All-Rocky Mountain Conference running back majoring in art history, as well as an avid movie fan, Steve was, as his father put it, "uniquely qualified to make football movies."

One of the things I remember very vividly about my father was that he had an incredible scrapbook chronicling an incredible career. He held the world record in the 100-meter freestyle and was an alternate on the Olympic team. He was a member of the 4x100-meter freestyle relay team. He played football at Blair Academy. He was actually a starring actor with the Olson and Johnson *and* Ritz Brothers comedy teams. Olson and Johnson were the forerunners to Martin and Lewis in the 1930s.

Dad had a collection of medals that was just unbelievable. They were framed and there must have been a bunch of them. As a kid who was somewhat of an athlete, it was so intimidating to see that. He had a trophy in his office at home that was three feet tall with a winged eagle atop it that said "World Record Holder, 100-Meter Freestyle: 50.4 seconds – Edwin Sabol." He actually broke Johnny Weissmuller's record.

So with that background and growing up in that household, you would think there would be a lot of pressure on me to perform as an athlete, but the thing that my father always stressed was to just do your best. Find something that you like to do and enjoy it; you don't have to come home with all the medals.

He was there to cheer me on and was always positive, especially when I played football on a high school team that won two or three games a year. There were other kids on my team whose fathers had been athletes, not at my dad's level, who were always very critical, and my father was exactly the opposite. He gave me nothing but encouragement.

He always had this belief that if you think you're right and you really believe in something, then you – as he used to say – go "balls and all." Go after it! It was an interesting philosophy because it played out in everything that my dad did.

If he went out shopping and saw something he liked, he would buy two of them. When Mercedes came out with a car that had gull-wing doors, he liked them so much he bought a pair. When we had horses, he bought two. His theory was, something will break or happen, so if you really love it, you'll have a backup.

That philosophy also worked its way into his personal life, whereby if he was sick and the doctor prescribed medicine, he would double it. His theory was to double everything. If they said one teaspoonful – take two. If they recommended two pills – take four. It was his feeling that you never hold back, and if you believe in something, you should put everything that you have behind it.

He has such an overwhelming joy for life. He would have one hobby after another and would pursue them all with fervor. If it wasn't horses, it was playing tennis, or whatever he was collecting, or airplanes. He decided he wanted to learn to fly – he's 88 years old and he still flies! It all goes back to living your dreams and following bliss. Don't hold back.

I've taken his passion to NFL Films. My father started it when he was 48 years old and I was 20. It's the only job I've ever known. But it's more than only a job – it's a vocation, it's a hobby, and in many ways it's my life. There are certain men who are lucky enough to be involved in something that they never look at as a job. That's me. Whenever I get a paycheck, I'm amazed. My job has been one 40-year labor of love, and my father made it all possible.

Maybe the greatest part of my dad is that he was so much fun and always made me laugh. To me, that's the most important thing in any relationship. Whether it's with a woman or a friend, the laughter is so important because there are so many things in life that you must face. There are struggles, adversities, and you have to be around someone who makes you laugh to keep it all in perspective.

My father has such a great sense of humor

He could fart louder than any man I've ever known.He could break wind at any time at a shattering pitch – it sounded like a washing machine breaking down. *Boom. Boom. BOOM!*

When I was young, we'd be in a crowded elevator and he would just rip a gigantic fart, and then he'd look at me and say, "I can't believe I raised a son to behave like that," and shake his head.

Everyone would look at me and think there's no way this little kid could have farted that loud. He would fart in meetings and in the office, and people can say it's repulsive or disgusting, but when he did it, it was just funny.

My father is the funniest guy I know.

ERIC SAPERSTON

ERIC SAPERSTON is the founder and president of Journey Productions, Inc. JPI's mission: "To bring people together through entertaining stories of wisdom, humor and inspiration."

Saperston earned his Bachelor of Arts degree in speech communications from San Diego State University and an Associate Arts diploma from Grossmont College, where he was student body president.

After college, Saperston bought a 1971 Volkswagen bus, took his golden retriever, Jack, and set out to follow The Grateful Dead and work a ski season in Aspen. Challenged by his mentor to make his trip more meaningful, Saperston decided to telephone some of the most powerful people in the world and invite them for a cup of coffee.

As his journey unfolded, Saperston meandered across the country, from Atlanta to Seattle, bought a video camera, shot 500 hours of footage and interviewed more than 200 people in search of wisdom and inspiration from the famous and not so famous. These interviews resulted in a development deal with Walt Disney Studios and ultimately became an award-winning feature film, *The Journey.*

Since 2001, tens of thousands of people have seen the film in theaters across America, and it has been screened for such corporations as Coca-Cola, Fast Company and Nike.

As a sought-after public speaker, Saperston has provided keynotes, workshops and leadership seminars to numerous universities, corporations and non-profit organizations.

Saperston's future plans include publishing a book and directing an upcoming feature film.

My dad is from Chicago. He is a real gruff, straight-up, no-bullshit kind of guy. He was a hard worker. My grandfather died when my father was young. Being the eldest son, he had to work during the day to be the breadwinner for the family. Then at night he put himself through school. He went to DePaul University and got a job working for a liquor distributor. He was very successful and explained to me and my siblings that he was on the fast-track to becoming a top executive.

My father says that when he met my mom, he knew she was the one. He took her bowling on their first date. He always says he lost the game but won the girl.

My mom was from a small town in Michigan, and she wanted to be a housewife. So the plan was for the two of them to come together and form this very traditional family. But five years into the marriage, when my dad was 28 years old, he had an induced stroke that left him paralyzed on the entire left side of his body. They already had two kids, my older brother and sister, and all of a sudden their world just collapsed.

My father suffered serious bouts of depression and had to go through rehab to learn how to use his body again. He even tried to kill himself. This was not the man my mom had married. All of a sudden she was subject to working. She went to school to become a nurse and ultimately became the main breadwinner for our family.

My dad never worked again.

Seven years later I was born. My father has been on disability my entire life, and because of the way benefits are paid in the United States, he cannot work again without losing his coverage. But he has coached baseball, been a Boy Scout leader, an Indian Guides leader and president of numerous homeowners associations. He is a very smart guy and has channeled the energy and intelligence he would have brought to the corporate world to other pursuits.

I was an angry kid. I did not like authority. I did not like people telling me what to do. My dad was angry, too. He had three kids to manage. When you grow up in a house like that and go to school, you find there are kids who have happier childhoods, easier home lives and a lot less tension. My parents fought in public and I often saw people stare in disgust towards my family. Other kids seemed to be living happier childhoods, and I was like, "Screw everybody." My life was chaos all the time. I was not easily controlled. I did not go to school and sit in the front row and pay attention to become an "A" student. It just did not call to me.

There was an inherent understanding in me that Dad had done everything society told him to do – went to school, got good grades, was kind to others and married a beautiful woman – but one day he woke up and it was all gone. So the law in my family is, there are no guarantees. Do not live your life like the world owes you anything. If you want something, focus and go get it. If it does not work out, do not be a victim about it.

I went to school on the outskirts of a wealthy town, so I met kids in school whose parents were wealthy, community leaders, judges and top business executives. These people were playing golf on the weekends with other movers and shakers and schlepping their sons along to make the contacts that could help them as their lives moved on. Dads were helping to position their sons to be in business. My dad was not positioning me to be in anything. I did not excel academically, I did not have any specific talent, no connections, and there was a looming sense of despair that the future did not hold a lot for me. After I finished school, I felt that if I wanted to be successful, I had better go seek out accomplished people. Maybe they would father me and take me under their wings.

So I bought a VW bus, took my golden retriever Jack and set out to interview the most powerful people in the world over coffee. At the time, I had no idea my trip would turn into a feature film.

Three-and-a-half years after my journey began, I found myself in Los Angeles, working with Disney and trying to wrap up our film.

Over lunch one afternoon, our producer at Disney asked our team this question. He said, "You all took this amazing journey, you met all these extraordinary people, so what did you learn from taking the adventure? What was the big epiphany?" My teammates seemed to get these great breakthroughs, but I was unable to see mine.

Then one of my teammates told me that out on the road I had been coaching and leading our team to victory. She wondered where all my core leadership beliefs came from. All of a sudden I started to cry and realized that the very man I was trying to avoid, trying to replace by asking all these other people for advice, had been with me the whole time. I traveled the continent in search of fatherly advice and the best advice had been by my side the whole time – my own father.

I guess Mark Twain was right when he said, "When I was a boy of 14, my father was so ignorant I could hardly stand to have the old man around. But when I got to be 21, I was astonished at how much the old man had learned in seven years."

At the core of my dad's being, he has not changed. He has grown a little softer, a little grayer and a little warmer over the years, but who he is has not changed very much at all. It is me who has changed. The greatest gift I got from my journey was seeing my father through new eyes.

Out on the road while making *The Journey,* I used to call him on the telephone and complain about how hard it was, who on my team I was in conflict with or wondering where I was going to get the next capital infusion. His response was, "Listen, you chose to do this, so quit complaining. Here, talk to your mom." His words were often harsh but always accurate.

I'm proud to say that with all the craziness of my youth, my parents have now been married for 44 years, and my sister has been married for 16 years and has three children. My brother is a top emergency room doctor and is recently married. I have been fortunate enough to make a feature film, start a production company and become a sought-after speaker to universities and organizations.

Bizarre as it may seem, our family is still together with all the crazy things that have happened. We love each other and have produced some great stuff. It is as if dad's paralysis ignited something in all of us – a sense of purpose, a drive and a need to accomplish. We also have no time for BS. It runs throughout our family. If the Saperstons care about you, you know we care about you. In my travels, I have learned that so many people have an inherent, debilitating fear. A fear of being judged, of being ostracized, of being loud, and often times that can really paralyze a person.

Well, my family was loud, my family was judged and my family was ostracized, but in many ways my father's paralysis gave us even more freedom to live a fully self-expressed life.

JEREMY SCHAAP

JEREMY SCHAAP is an ESPN host and national correspondent, based in New York since September 1998. He is one of the two hosts of *Outside the Lines,* is a frequent guest host and panelist on *The Sports Reporters,* and is one of the two hosts of ESPN's acclaimed *SportsCentury* series.

"Jeremy draws the down and dirty assignments," Phil Mushnick writes in *TV Guide,* "from tracking down Mike Tyson, John Rocker and Darryl Strawberry to conducting the first TV sit-down with Bobby Knight after Knight was sacked at Indiana. But Jeremy deserves what he gets. As these assignments have proven, he's good at it. Real good."

In 2001, Schaap was honored by the Columbia University Graduate School of Journalism for his two-part story on a white Florida high school football coach whose use of a racial epithet sparked a furor in the community.

Schaap has won five Emmy awards – four for his work on *Outside the Lines* and one as a feature producer for *SportsCenter.* His work has been published in *Sports Illustrated, ESPN the Magazine, Time magazine, Parade magazine, TV Guide* and *The New York Times.*

Born August 23, 1969, Schaap is a native of New York City and a 1991 graduate of Cornell University. He is the son of award-winning journalist Dick Schaap.

Jeremy Schaap has followed his father's footsteps into his chosen career. Those footsteps are the size of snowshoes. His father is the legendary Dick Schaap, who has been a defining sport reporter for almost 50 years. Jeremy remembers Dick as a journalist, a commentator and, most importantly, as a dad.

"My father saw Bill Mazeroski end the 1960 World Series with a home run; he saw Jerry Kramer throw the block that won the Ice Bowl; he saw Muhammad Ali and Joe Frazier pummel each other in Manila; and he saw Reggie Jackson hit one home run in Game 6 of the 1977 World Series. Jackson, of course, hit three home runs to help the Yankees beat the Dodgers in that game. My father saw him hit the first, off Burt Hooton. When Jackson hit his second, my father was at a concession stand buying me popcorn. And when Jackson hit his third, my father was buying me a soda.

"Eventually, he forgave me. I think.

"A year after Jackson's big night, my father took me to Fenway Park for a one-game playoff between the Red Sox and the Yankees. I was too young to sit in the press box, so he asked some players if any of them had spare tickets. 'Sure,' said the Yankees' shortstop Bucky Dent. 'You can have mine.' That's how we came to be sitting in Bucky Dent's seats when he hit the game-winning three-run home run that Boston fans still cry over.

"I was privileged to spend those moments with my father, to tag along at Super Bowls, Olympics and World Series. But the moments I remember best were the quieter ones watching him at work. For me, my father is a sound: the steady click of his fingers on the keyboard, a cadence I remember awakening to from earliest childhood.

"There was always something that had to be written, usually at six in the morning. A book, a television script, a magazine article, a theater review, a radio or TV commentary. He loved writing. My father often said that when you love your job as much as he did, it wasn't work. That's why I wanted to be a sports reporter – I wanted to have as much fun as he had.

"I would love to go with him to one more game at Lambeau Field or Madison Square Garden. But what I'd really like is to wake up once more to that sound, the clack-clack of the keyboard – the soundtrack of his life.

"In television, his debut was inauspicious. The day my father went on the air for the first time in 1971 – at WNBC-TV in New York – he was 36, and reading off a TelePrompTer. He knew so little about television that he had no idea the red light indicated which camera to look at. He was nervous and looked it.

"The New York *Daily News* reviewed Dick Schaap's sportscasting debut this way: 'He sounded like he wasn't going to get through it. Unfortunately, he did.'

"Clearly, Walter Cronkite's job was safe. But within a few years, my father had mastered television, as he had previously mastered magazines (senior editor at *Newsweek* at 26), newspapers (city editor of the *New York Herald Tribune* at 29), and books (co-author of *Instant Replay*, at the time the best-selling sports book ever, at 34).

"My father's television success depended almost entirely on his mastery of the language and his strength of personality. His voice was untrained. His delivery was far from smooth. He never learned to fake a smile. But his writing talent was unmatched and his presence, especially as he grew older, was formidable. I know he would groan at the cliché, but ultimately his success was a victory of substance over style. He was all substance.

"If there was a guiding principle in his work, it was his belief that the story was never about him. He hated the first person – or at least the casual, self-aggrandizing, nearly reflexive use of it by today's generation of television journalists.

"My father liked to say that he collected people, and certainly his collection included many of the most important figures of the last 50 years. But it also included hundreds of people less famous but equally as interesting. Many of his best stories were about virtual unknowns. The story he was perhaps most proud of was a *20/20* profile of Tom Waddell, an Olympic decathlete who founded the Gay Games and was dying of AIDS. He also told wonderful stories about Lebanese skiers, a man wrongfully imprisoned for murder, a Division III football player who built and ran a miniature golf course. I could go on.

"My father never took the easy way out. He was never lazy, or glib or cruel. He never made jokes at the expense of his subjects, the people who agreed to allow him into their lives.

"Somehow he always found the essential decency of his subjects – if there was any to be found – and honored them with his words.

"Fifteen months before my father died, Bob Knight, his old friend, told me during an interview, 'You've got a long way to go to be as good as your dad.'

"He was right. I think just about everyone has a long way to go to be as good as my dad."

BOB SCHIEFFER

BOB SCHIEFFER, broadcast journalism's most experienced Washington reporter, has been anchor and moderator of *Face The Nation,* CBS News' Sunday public affairs broadcast, since May 1991. He also serves as CBS News' chief Washington correspondent.

He has won many broadcast news awards, including five Emmys and two Sigma Delta Chi Awards. In 2002 the National Press Foundation chose Schieffer as its Broadcaster of the Year. He has been a principal anchor for CBS News since 1973, when he was named anchor of the CBS Sunday Night News.

He began his professional career in 1957 while still a student at Texas Christian University, where he received a B.A. in journalism and English in 1959. He is an Air Force veteran. He has co-authored several books, including *Acting President,* a book about Ronald Reagan published in 1989.

Schieffer was born February 25, 1937, in Austin, Texas. He and his wife reside in Washington, D.C. They have two daughters.

My dad was a hardworking, honest man who grew up during the Depression on a dairy farm on the outskirts of Austin.

As a boy he loved to build things and always had a knack for math and hoped to attend Texas A&M and become an engineer. But times were hard and he and his brothers never got to college. After high school they went to work to pay taxes on the farm. Otherwise, the bank would have foreclosed.

When he and my mother married, he worked behind the counter at an Austin lumber yard. My mother's father had driven one of the lumber yard's delivery trucks, but when the Depression came he was laid off, and her brother, who was in the sixth grade, quit school and went to work in a drug store. That brother was her family's sole support. As part of his pay, he was allowed to take home a quart of milk and a box of crackers each day. The crackers were crumbled into bowls of the milk and that became the family's supper.

As it was with most of their generation, my mother and father were frugal, inventive people. They had to be. They had little money to spend but they found ways to live on it, and their word was always good.

During World War II, my dad got a job working for a Fort Worth construction company that was building a bomb factory in Waco, a small town in Central Texas. Waco was only 90 miles from our home of Austin, but it was no small feat for Dad to move us there. We had a 1932 Ford, and the tires were so bald he was afraid to drive it on the highway. It was my grandfather who found the solution. Grampa Schieffer put his own car up on concrete blocks, removed the tires and put them on our car. He piled our old tires in the back of dad's brother Richie's car. Then we all set out for Waco, us in our car, Grampa and Richie in his car. Once we got to Waco, they switched tires again, and Grampa and Richie drove back to Austin with Grampa's tires. We spent the rest of the war driving around on those old bald tires.

We lived in Waco while the defense plant was built, and when that job was done we moved on to Fort Worth, where the construction firm was building housing for workers at the aircraft factory we knew as the "bomber plant."

I started first grade in Fort Worth, and then daddy got drafted and we moved back to Austin to live with Mother's parents. Dad passed his physical and I remember how proud he was and how proud the family was. He didn't want to leave us, but I remember him saying, "We all have to do our duty."

I restarted first grade in Austin. We planned to live there with Mom's parents until Dad came back from the war, but he never went. President Roosevelt decided the war effort did not need men of a certain age who had children. So the construction firm sent him to Houston to do work on a shipyard they were building. We couldn't find a house to rent, so after living for several weeks in a motel, I was enrolled in yet another school. I was there only a matter of days, but with no place to live, the construction firm told us to return to Fort Worth, where work on emergency housing for bomber plant workers continued. I was enrolled in yet another school. I was barely through the first half of first grade and had already attended four schools.

My dad didn't say much – Mom did the talking in our family – but he came to the school to pick me up on the day I got my first report card. He looked at it and seemed genuinely pleased.

I can still remember those words: "Bobby, this is straight As. I'm proud of you, son."

I wasn't sure what straight As meant, but I knew I had made my dad happy. That was all I needed to know.

When the war ended, my father and some fellow construction company workers formed their own contracting firm. I remember hearing people say, "Johnny Schieffer is a good man to do business with. When he tells you something, that's how it is."

I wasn't sure what that meant either, but it made me proud to hear somebody say something nice about him, and I was as proud of him as he was of me.

I always wanted to be a baseball player. I didn't get to play much in high school but when I got to TCU, I made the freshman team and started the first five games of the season. One afternoon dad came out to see me play. I was a catcher and had a good day, got a hit and threw out a couple of runners who tried to steal a base on me. My mom had always been the one to go to ball games, since dad worked long hours and was never around much. But he had come to see me that day and afterward he said, "You know, Bobby, you might make a ball player after all." I got hurt after that and couldn't finish out the season but I didn't really care. I had finally made the starting lineup and my dad had seen me play a couple of games.

Dad died the next year, and I was glad he had come to the ballpark that day to see me play. After he died, I wished we had talked more. But as I look back on it now, I realize that he was talking to me all along. He just didn't always put it in words. He taught me to be honest by being honest. He taught me to work hard by working hard. He taught me to understand that I had an obligation to my country by doing his duty. He taught me to hang in there by hanging in there. And most of all, he let me know that he was proud of me.

My dad didn't talk much, but he said all the right things.

In March 2005, Bob Schieffer was named the interim anchor for the CBS Evening News, replacing his long time colleague, Dan Rather, and escalating him to the pinnacle of network news.

STEPHANIE SCHWABE

DR. STEPHANIE SCHWABE, underwater cave explorer and scientist, received her Master's degree from Mississippi State University and earned her Ph.D. from the University of Bristol in England. In addition, she graduated from the University of Queensland law school in Australia and is now registered as a barrister and mediator with the Supreme Court of Queensland. She is currently teaching geology at the College of Charleston, SC, while she gets her research base set up again in the Bahamas. She is the founder and director of the Rob Palmer Blue Holes Foundation, based in the Bahamas as well.

Schwabe has been diving for nearly 25 years in the Bahamian blue holes and the recently discovered black holes, Florida aquifers, in the UK and Australia. Her scientific exploration into the underwater caves of the Bahamas became the subject of her Ph.D., which is focused on the geomicrobiology of these environments. Her law degree is focused on international environmental law with the purpose of trying to protect these special underground environments.

She has been a part of 20 scientific expeditions to the Bahamas, subject for masters theses and doctoral research, exploration and major film work for German, British and American television. She is a subject of the book *Women of Discovery*.

She was married to British diver, explorer and author Robert John

Palmer, who died in a diving accident in 1997 while in Egypt.

Schwabe is also a fellow of the Royal Geographical Society in London and a National Fellow of the Explorers Club in New York.

I grew up in a household where beatings were memorable events. The most unfortunate part of this is that they were doled out a bit too frequently and seemed, for the most part, to have no justification except that I was a convenient target. Mental abuse from my father was generously offered up as well, to the point that I actually believed that any failure on my part confirmed my lack of cerebral capacity. This became a problem that took four degrees and 25 years to cure.

My father, who volunteered the heavy hands and the emotional abuse, is today still actively involved in research. He has two DDSs – one from the University of Hamburg, Germany, and the other from the University of Iowa. He has a Ph.D. in biochemistry, which is where his passions lie, besides sailing. His genius, along with his passion for research, landed him a teaching position at Harvard for quite a few years. When an offer came to teach and do research at the Medical University of South Carolina in Charleston, the weather and the beauty of the city made for an easy decision to leave Boston and move to Charleston. He has been there ever since.

For a scientist with a mind like my father's, ignorance, deadwood, or whatever one calls it is the most irritating thing. Unfortunately, this is a trait not unusual in people like him. You never hear about Einstein "and all his friends," but one does read about his anti-social behavior and lack of affection for his family members. It is an interesting trait because these people are so unemotional about family events, but when it comes to thinking or science they lose their heads and become tyrants. Procreation was something that you had to prove you could do, but once that dirty deed was over, it was back to the workbench, leaving the gentler sex to handle the rest of it. That is my father in a nutshell.

Regardless of what I think of him as a person, he is a genius of amazing proportions, and the work he has done, the way he thinks about things, the information he has in his mind and his way of explaining things is amazing. In that sense, he is very cool.

I was fascinated with him as a kid. I remember thinking, this man is bigger than life, despite his somewhat detached nature with me. I wanted to follow him around to see what he was doing. When school was out during the summer months, he would take me to the laboratory and teach me to clean the glassware. This saved on the babysitting bill. To a kid of preteen years, this was a pretty cool place to hang out. All that glassware and stuff on the shelves was a great wonder to me. When my father had a bit of time, he would teach me how to measure melting points of certain chemicals. I was so eager to please him – and to show him that I could do something right – that if the lab had caught on fire before the melting point had been reached, I would not have left. Okay, maybe I wasn't so smart, but I so badly wanted his approval.

Although his cerebral nature explains his introverted behavior, other factors played a significant role in forming his personality. He had a very emotionally abusive father who did horrible things to him, and whilst I can feel sorry for him, having experienced the same, at age 46 I am nothing like him along that line. I think I was more like him when I first left home at 17, but I was made aware of my behavior and – having been the recipient of meanness – I made the choice that this was not the correct way to interact with people, even those who cannot chew and walk at the same time. If I could make this kind of major adjustment, why couldn't my father? Answer: he didn't care enough to change, so that put things into perspective for me. Either get over it or let him make an emotional mess of me. I got over it. Today I can say, without any guilt, that I love my father and would do whatever it takes to protect him, but I don't like him and that is okay.

Strangely enough, however, life is doling out its form of justice on my father, and this indeed is a tragedy. Here is a man with so much to share and so much to say, yet he has no audience. I wouldn't wish this situation on anybody. Talk about a silent death. I have very little doubt that one day his name will go down in scientific history, but the possibility of his enjoying some acclaim for his work while he is still alive is not likely, and this is where I feel sorry for him. He is a bird trapped in a golden cage.

Fundamentally, I am not really a people person. As a kid in the States who couldn't speak a word of English, facing my father's detachment from me, being raped repeatedly by a half brother, and having to face the "fact" that I probably would not amount to anything worthy, the world was not a nice place for me. I was so terrified and shy of people that it was pathetic. Fortunately, however, I slowly learned to interact with the world, even to the point that I agreed at the age of 34 to marry my late husband. He taught me that I was capable of loving another human being. That, indeed, was a great gift to me. That meant that I was not so abnormal.

My father and I do have some similarities. We are both very passionate about things in which we are involved. We are not people who give up. We do not let go of an idea or pursuit because it gets difficult. We are both in science up to our armpits. We both love racing sailboats, and we love to win. Another way in which we are much alike is our mannerisms – how we grin or smile or say certain words. We are two very strong people who chose a different path to achieve similar goals.

I don't feel sorry for myself and I never have. I consider myself, despite everything, to be very lucky. I have achieved intellectual freedom, I am secure in who I am, I am confident and I know that there is nothing in this world that I can't do, within reason. I could have had an alcoholic or a drug addict for a father, or one that burned me with his cigarettes, but I didn't. So no matter how dark times got for me, I always kept in mind that someone else out in the world had it a lot worse than I did. I guess this is what is called "life," and I am lucky to be a part of it.

WENDY SELIG-PRIEB

WENDY SELIG-PRIEB is the only female chairman of a Major League Baseball club. She was born in Milwaukee on March 18, 1960. She graduated from Tufts University *magna cum laude* in 1982 with a bachelor's degree in political science. She graduated *magna cum laude* from Marquette University while earning her *juris doctorate* from their law school. Her passion and leadership have been vital to the Brewers since 1990, when she joined the club as General Counsel. In September 1992 she assumed more responsibility of day-to-day operations of the club when her father, Allan H. "Bud" Selig, became chairman of baseball's Executive Council. On August 4, 1998, she replaced him as president and CEO of the Milwaukee Brewers when he accepted the position of commissioner of Major League Baseball.

Selig-Prieb is also very active in the community. She is currently a member of the Board of Directors of the Child Abuse Prevention Fund and United Way of Greater Milwaukee. Since 1998 she has served as the honorary chair for the March of Dimes WalkAmerica, and she is co-chair of the YWCA's Circle of Women Luncheon.

Street and Smith's *Sports Business Journal* ranked her among the most powerful women in sports for three consecutive years and included her in its inaugural "40 under 40" list in 1999.

Selig-Prieb is married to Laurel Prieb. They have a daughter,

Natalie, and reside in Fox Point, Wisconsin.

My father has been a great leader and accomplished many things. There is no question we would not have Major League baseball in Milwaukee if not for him. There is also no question that my father's leadership and vision have made baseball an even better and more popular game. While he loves the history and traditions of baseball, my father has recognized that changes like an additional round of playoffs, the wildcard and inter-league play only make the sport better. Most importantly, he has made a commitment to restore competitive balance to Major League baseball so that all fans have hope and faith in their team every spring.

My father is as hard working as anyone I know, and I often say he is fortunate because his avocation and vocation are one and the same. While my father is very serious and hardworking, there is no one who is more fun to be around, because he has a tremendous sense of humor, a wealth of stories to tell and the ability to tell them well.

When he graduated from college, my father wanted to be a history professor. But his father convinced him to try business for a year, and from there his career took off. I have said many times that if my father had become the history professor he wanted to be, or a doctor or lawyer or engineer, I may not have followed in his footsteps. I might not have been as interested in hanging around the office with him, because hanging around the office meant hanging around the ballpark, and that is a lot of fun! What child would pass up that opportunity?

As a parent, my father always encouraged us to be the best that we could be. He often speaks of lessons he learned from his parents, and he has now passed those lessons on to me. When I was growing up, school, and education generally, was taken very seriously, just as it had been during my father's upbringing because my grandmother was a teacher. People often ask me if I want my daughter to go into baseball. The answer is, as I tell her every day when I kiss her goodbye and send her off to school, I want her to be the best Natalie Prieb she can be.

That really is what my father instilled in me and what his parents instilled in him. So while many people think I am lucky because my father was Bud Selig, president of the Milwaukee Brewers or now Commissioner of Baseball, I know I was lucky because my father taught me what is really important in life.

The greatest lesson that I learned from my father is that it is okay to dream big dreams; however, it is tenacity and perseverance that make those dreams come true. In a way, if my parents had sat me down and tried to teach me a lesson like that, I probably would have listened, then said "Okay," and gone on my way to the next thing. But the way I learned this lesson was by watching what my father did when the Braves left Milwaukee in 1965. He began by forming an organization whose sole purpose was to bring Major League baseball back to Milwaukee. All I knew was that my father was passionate about the cause, he had an unwavering belief that it would happen and that there were many people in our own community who did not believe it would happen.

My father, the eternal optimist, always believed he was close. In 1969, Major League baseball expanded by adding teams in Kansas City, Seattle, San Diego and Montreal. My father likes to tell of when he was at the meeting where the teams were announced. He was very hopeful and believed one of the teams would be awarded to Milwaukee. I was nine at the time and I still remember him saying he was going out of town for a very important meeting. He recounts when Warren Giles, who was then the National League president, announced that the two new National League cities would be San Diego and Montreal. My father saw Mr. Giles' mouth forming an *M* sound and he was sure it was Milwaukee. It was not!

A year later the Seattle Pilots were in bankruptcy court, and my father and his partners were successful in buying that team and moving them to Milwaukee, and they became the Brewers.

It was by watching that experience for five years, and seeing the way my father was laser-beam focused on his mission, that I learned the importance of having a dream and coupling it with perseverance and tenacity. It was a great lesson to learn, and to this day it has had a meaningful impact upon me.

No one has had more influence on me than my father. I have constantly learned and taken so many positive personality traits from him. I feel fortunate because as I was developing a love of baseball, my father not only taught me about the game but also about the business. He has had a tremendous amount of success, so who would not want to learn from someone like that? I am just that much more fortunate that he happens to be my father.

DONNA SHIRLEY

DONNA SHIRLEY, director of the Mars Exploration Program, was raised in Wynnewood, Oklahoma, population 2,500. Her parents encouraged her academic studies, but most people were surprised when the very small girl took an intense interest in flying airplanes. Her father and mother encouraged her, and before she was out of her teens, Donna was soloing and earning her pilot's license. She entered college in 1958 expressly to study aeronautic engineering when engineering schools were still all-male bastions. From her early teens she had been fascinated by science fiction and dreamed of exploring Mars. Her first post-graduate assignments led her into the technology that has played a role in the exploration of the Red Planet.

After graduation, Shirley worked as a specification writer before winning a job with NASA's Jet Propulsion Laboratory in 1966. She worked on what was to have been the first lander on Mars before it was cancelled in 1968. For the next 30 years she continued her association with planetary exploration, including Mars research. That devotion came to splendid fruition on July 4, 1997,when the world watched the Mars Pathfinder and the Sojourner Rover successfully land on Mars. Two months later the Mars Global Surveyor successfully went into orbit around the Red Planet. Not only were these events two of the U.S. space program's most visible successes, they may also provide some of the most important scientific data of the 20th and 21st centuries.

Donna Shirley has written an autobiography, *Managing Martians: The Extraordinary Story of a Woman's Lifelong Quest to Get to Mars — and of the Team Behind the Space Robot That Has Captured the Imagination of the World.* It's the story of her life from her childhood in Oklahoma to managing the Mars Exploration Program at the Jet Propulsion Laboratory.

For some years, Shirley has taught a course called *Managing Creativity*, based on her experience at NASA and JPL. After leaving NASA in 1998, she wrote an on-line book called *Managing Creativity: A Practical Guide to Inventing, Developing and Producing Innovative Products.* She recently retired (for the second time) as Assistant Dean of Engineering at the University of Oklahoma.

Ms. Shirley has a daughter and lives in Seattle, Washington, where she is the director of the Science Fiction Museum.

My father was a physician born in Silver Springs, Texas, in 1910. His parents actually lived in Oklahoma and he was the younger of two sons. His great-grandfather would have been chief of the Chickasaw Nation had they not been driven over the "Trail of Tears" from Mississippi to Oklahoma. But when they decided they were a nation and needed a leader, he was elected their first governor.

His grandfather was a fellow named Noah Lael, who was Pennsylvania Dutch from North Carolina, fought in the Civil War as a teenager and ended up in Texas working for the stage line shoeing horses. While traveling for the stage line in the late 1870s, he met Lucy Harris, the youngest daughter of Cyrus Harris, in southern Oklahoma. He married her and they had two children. Unfortunately, during her third birth, she and the baby both died. Noah never re-married but lived the rest of his life on a ranch near Wynnewood, where he brought up his son and daughter. His daughter was my grandmother, Rushie.

Rushie married a man named Thornton Shirley and had my uncle. In a move unusual for the time, they got divorced, then remarried, had my father and divorced again. My father was raised by my grandmother and his stepfather, who was a prosperous farmer and owner of the local cotton gin. Their property also had enough oil and gas deposits that they were able to send my father to medical school.

He was the quarterback on the Wynnewood High School football team but was not very big, only five feet eight or so. When he went off to the University of Oklahoma, he wanted to play football so he wouldn't have to enroll in ROTC. But when he walked onto the field, as he put it, he was "surrounded by elephants," so he kept walking right across the football field to the ROTC office. That was 1925 and the ROTC cadets rode horses in the cavalry. He really did not enjoy it, and it was the only course in which he made a B. This came about because while the platoon he was leading was marching in review and pulling a mounted cannon, my father ordered a too-sharp turn, which caused the cannon to catch the edge of the reviewing stand and pull it down. All the officers were thrown in a heap, after which my father spent a great deal of time soaping saddles. Maybe he should have stuck with the elephants on the football field.

After medical school he met my mother, who was the daughter of a Methodist minister. They were married in 1938 and moved to Pauls Valley, Oklahoma, where I was born in July of 1941. That was soon followed by the attack on Pearl Harbor in December. Because my father was very nearsighted, he was not allowed to enter the military until 1944, when they were really desperate for doctors. The story goes that when they asked him to read the eye chart on the wall, he answered, "What chart?" They said, "You pass," and that's how he joined the Navy. He bobbed around the Pacific for a couple of years on a supply ship, got shipwrecked during a typhoon but was never shot at. After the war he went to Japan as part of the occupation, and then returned to Wynnewood to practice medicine.

He wanted me to be a doctor because he was a devoted, country general practitioner. He was always getting up at two in the morning delivering babies and going off to weird places in the country to take care of people. One time he went out to this very remote area – it took him a couple of hours to get there – to see a man who said he was very desperately ill. When he got there and started the examination, he said, "What seems to be the matter?" to which the man replied, "Piles," or hemorrhoids. My father asked, "How long have you had them?" and he said, "About 40 years." He was just a lonely man who wanted someone to pay attention to him. My father was as much company as physician.

He was a very nice guy and much beloved in the town. He liked to play golf and go hunting with his buddies for quail and squirrels — not exactly big game. He was one of those leading citizens, as small-town doctors often are. Everybody loved him and said he was instrumental in the whole life of the community.

On the other hand, he was always tired and never got enough sleep. He smoked even though he knew better and never got any exercise. He also took it very hard when he would lose a patient – he took it personally and it started to wear him down. He wanted to save everybody. He took to sleeping in his underwear as opposed to his pajamas so he could get dressed more quickly. He would just put his pants on and go. Finally, at the much-too-young age of 58, he died of a heart attack.

That was not the way I wanted to live my life. In some ways, I learned how to live by not acting like him. But in others, I am just like him. I tend to work too hard and have trouble saying "no" to things like non-profit boards. I come from a long line of leading citizens on both sides of my family. In addition to my descent from a tribal governor on my father's side, my mother's preacher father was famous for raising money for building Methodist churches in Oklahoma, and he helped develop the state's educational program shortly after statehood.

I share a number of other characteristics with my father. He cared deeply about people, was very funny and really wanted to make a difference. He loved to make people laugh, especially my younger sister and me. When we were little he would tell us stories about families of seals that wore flipper mittens, and other stories about woodland animals, complete with sounds. The stories were very charming. When we were driving he would wiggle his mouth around in an amusing way, which was reflected in the rear-view mirror so that only my sister and I could see him from the back seat. My mother would be sitting beside him and would never see him do it. But my sister and I would burst out laughing, and just as my mother would turn to look, he would stop. She could never catch him. I like to think I have his sense of humor, and I told my daughter stories of "Alice Astronaut" like my father told me about the seals.

He also kept learning new things all his life. He would take medical correspondence courses in subjects like hypnotism, which he practiced on my sister and me. There are many such memories that had an influence on me.

The most important thing he did for me was to recognize my aptitude and support my ambitions. I know he wanted me to be a doctor, but when I told him that I wanted to be an engineer, he did not twist my arm or try to force me in another direction. He was always very supportive of everything I tried. He understood, though he didn't share, my fascination with flight and actually gave me flying lessons for my fifteenth birthday, and he continued paying for them until I graduated from college.

He lived to see only the early part of my career, but I think my success did and would make him happy, and that is all I could ask.

GERRY SPENCE

GERRY SPENCE was born and educated in rural Wyoming, where he has practiced law for nearly 50 years. He has spent his lifetime representing the poor, the injured and the forgotten against large corporations and the government. He has tried and won many cases of national interest, including the Karen Silkwood case, the defense of Randy Weaver at Ruby Ridge, the defense of Imelda Marcos, the case against *Penthouse Magazine* for Miss Wyoming, and other important criminal and civil trials. He has never lost a criminal case. He has not lost a civil case since 1969. He has had more multi-million dollar verdicts without an intervening loss than any lawyer in America.

Spence is the founder of the Trial Lawyers College and is the author of 12 books, including the best-seller *How to Argue and Win Every Time,* as well as *From Freedom to Slavery, O.J.: The Last Word, The Making of a Country Lawyer, Murder and Madness, A Boy's Summer, With Justice for None, Give Me Liberty!, Gunning for Justice, Gerry Spence's Wyoming* and *Half-Moon and Empty Stars.*

He is also a noted photographer and poet.

❧

At 12 I became a man, because then I was old enough to go with my father on my first hunt. To symbolize my passage into manhood, he bought me a government surplus 30:40 Springfield rifle, the one used in the Spanish-American war. It cost something like seven dollars, had a stock that extended nearly to the end of its barrel, and came in the mail with the cosmoline still in the barrel. My father installed a one-dollar peep sight at the breach, and after having sighted it in, and after I had been thoroughly instructed on how to shoot from both prone and sitting positions, off we went one early crisp October morning to hunt deer. We hunted to eat. I never tasted beef until I was past 15.

My father contended that the Wyoming Game and Fish Commission set the opening day of deer season so that the rich, who didn't have to work for a living, could enjoy the hunt unencumbered by the horde of working men who would otherwise be taking to the field. In those hard times men worked six days a week. On a Sunday, the second day of deer season, my father drove us in our Model A Ford to Little Goose Creek, where he said he knew of a secret herd.

My excitement made it hard to breathe. I couldn't talk and my father wasn't one to say much either. I remember him slapping my leg and smiling at me. The leg slap meant we were together, a couple of men on a hunt, which was among the highest callings of the species. To my father, hunting trumped churching. A man ought not suffer stuffy, man-made churches in deer season when he could go into God's own perfect church, the out-of-doors, and in the process bring home some venison.

It was just getting light, say, a little past six, when we arrived at Little Goose Creek. Suddenly my father brought the Ford to an abrupt halt. He nodded toward a grove of quaking aspens, and there, in the dim early morning, I could make out the white rumps of a small herd of mule deer. My father eased out of the Ford and silently beckoned me to do the same. With a finger to his lips he admonished me to close my door quietly. He lifted his rifle from the back seat and handed me mine. At the barbed wire fence, we slipped our unloaded rifles under first. Then we crawled through and loaded our guns. I was shaking. He looked at me and whispered, "It's O.K., it's just buck fever." But the deer and the cold morning and buck fever were not the only cause of my trembling. There, on the very fence post where we crawled through, was a sign that read, "No hunting or trespassing. Violators will be prosecuted."

Following the outer edge of the aspen grove and in a crouch, my father walked quickly toward the grazing deer. When we were about 50 yards from the herd, he eased down and made a motion for me to do likewise. We lingered for a moment, our breaths making those small clouds like steam from an almost boiling kettle. Then my father leaned over and whispered, "Pick out a dry doe." There were no bucks in the herd. A dry doe was one that had no fawn at its side. I looked and quickly chose the largest doe in the herd. He whispered further instructions. "Take your sitting position. Be sure your gun is off safe." I did as he said. I was taking small short breaths like a pup panting in July. "Now aim just above her elbow – that's where the heart lies. Okay. Now hold your breath. Don't close your eyes. Hold steady. Now squeeze the trigger nice and slow."

Then the explosion!

The doe fell like a dropped sack, rolled over on her back, and kicked at the air a few times in death spasms. My father ran to her, I a couple of yards behind. He pulled his hunting knife from its scabbard, sliced her belly open, and with great skill and dispatch extracted her entrails. Then he handed me his rifle to carry while he quickly drug the carcass to the car.

Once back in the Ford, the doe safely in the back seat on a canvas cover, and the old wreck rattling toward home again, we were finally able to speak.

"That was a good shot, son," he said.

I was proud. But something was bothering me. Finally I asked, "Dad, what about that No Trespassin' sign? Weren't we violatin' the law?"

"Well, son," he said, "that land belongs to a rich English remittance man," as if that were a complete answer. A remittance man, as he later explained, is a son of some wealthy lord in Britain where primogeniture prevailed so that the eldest son inherited the entire estate of the parents. So what do you do with the middle kids? You get them out of the way by shipping them off to Wyoming or some other frontier, give them enough money to buy up the choice land along wonderful trout streams, and send them a check every year – their remittances – to live on.

"But how come we trespassed?"

"Well, son," he said looking down the road as if he saw a vision, "the rich man owns the land. But the *people* own the deer." He looked over at me as if I should understand. That insight didn't mean much to me at the time, but later as I became a part of the legal system, I learned that the law is often not just. It is just the law.

"Weren't you afraid they'd catch us?" I asked.

"Those kind never get up that time of the mornin'," he said.

And something else I learned. That doe I shot didn't have a tooth in her head. She was old and tough, and although my mother pounded her steaks until they were nearly hamburger, her meat remained stringy and nearly inedible. "Besides," my father said as I chewed endlessly on a piece of her steak, "chewing is good for your jaws." Then he grinned and winked at my mother.

But the unyielding principle my father taught us was that we eat what we kill. And we ate every last ounce of that old doe right down to her liver and her heart. Wasting any part of her would have been a sin of the worst order — something approaching murder, although there was no law that said you had to eat what you killed. The doe had given up her life to us. There was a holiness about that they didn't teach in church.

I learned from my father that ethics exist independent of the law. I've never needed the law to tell me what was right or wrong, nor the church nor any guru nor anyone else. Often those who render judgments against us are wrong. Although we are bound by the law, and by the values of a decent society, I learned from my father that the final judgments on the choices we make are judgments rendered by the self in a courtroom in which the self is on trial, and the self – a most formidable judge and jury – hands down its verdict.

ANNE STEVENS

ANNE STEVENS is group vice president, Canada, Mexico and South America, for Ford Motor Company. She is Ford's first female group vice president.

Stevens serves on the board of the UAW Family Service and Learning Center, the Lockheed Martin board of directors, the board of trustees at Drexel University and an advisory board for a graduate business program at Northwestern University. Stevens was named to *Fortune* magazine's 2001 and 2002 list of "50 Most Powerful Women In Business," *Crain's* magazine's "Most Influential Women" and "Michigan's 95 Most Powerful Women" by *Corp!* magazine.

Born in Reading, Pennsylvania, Stevens holds a bachelor's degree in mechanical and materials engineering from Drexel University in Philadelphia and did graduate work at Rutgers University in New Brunswick, New Jersey.

Forty years ago, Reading was a charming city made up of many strong ethnic neighborhoods – each, of course, with its share of churches and bars. At one time there were actually more bars than churches, so most people were in good spirits! It was a time in America when "inclusion"–

or lack of it – was the fiber of our everyday lives. Various ethnic groups, races and religions lived within a stone's throw of one another and were encouraged to meld their differences. The elderly received support from the young, who ran their errands, listened to their life stories or just passed the time chatting with them. Our homes were small and didn't have air conditioning. In the summer, we all socialized on the front porch – the "stoop troop," as we endearingly called it.

When I think of my father, Paul Alvin Anthony Haage, I recall a man who never spoke disparagingly about anyone. He was the most inclusive person I have ever known. I learned about the strength of diversity from him at a very early age. He recognized the contributions of all people, regardless of physical, social or economic status. This character trait, which probably defied conventional thinking at the time, can probably be traced to his own heritage and the lessons his parents taught him. He provided me a steady foundation and perspective upon which to build a career and a life. Little did I know that those lessons would later prepare me to inspire others and build winning teams at major corporations. He taught me that we were all capable of so much more; it is just a matter of expecting it from ourselves.

This early awareness of the strength in diversity wasn't the only valuable lesson that I have carried with me throughout nearly every facet of my life. My dad also taught me never to equate knowledge or intelligence with position. Some of the smartest people are often on the front line. I have applied that lesson to my life and career, and I understand that as a business leader, I've reached my pinnacle when I've created an inspired, high-performing and aligned team; a team that not only performs well but also has a sense of camaraderie and mutual caring.

My father also taught me that strong, positive relationships could be formed only through mutual respect, honesty and the willingness to continuously learn and grow. We cannot sustain ourselves as leaders if we are not committed to lifelong learning. With time, you grow obsolete and ineffective. Imagine a leader today with no computer skills or knowledge of the Web!

He believed that if you never fail, you aren't trying hard enough – you aren't going for the stretch of your abilities and you will never maximize your opportunity to learn. He believed that the biggest sin we can commit in life is to not fully develop and use all of the talent and potential that we are born with. Knowledge is power, but only in using it will you ever have true power in life. He would tell me that sometimes, opportunity will knock only once. You have to learn to recognize it and be ready to take the risk.

He always pushed me to my limits, but he was always there to teach me and coach me when I stumbled. He would often remind me that anything is possible if you work hard and are persistent in success as well as in failure.

I can recall one incident that speaks volumes about the kind of man he was, and about his belief in me. When I was very young, I wanted to go fishing at the beach. Unfortunately, my dad did not know how to fish and had no equipment. So with a dollar in my pocket, I went into a fishing shop, bought some hand line, a few hooks and line weights. I awoke at 5:00 a.m. the next morning and walked to the beach to dig up clams before the sunbathing crowd arrived. Then with fishing gear, bait, a pail in hand and enough determination to catch a whale, I climbed out on a long rock jetty to fish. After hours of watching the waves, just as my hopes began to dwindle, I finally managed to catch two eight-inch fish. As I turned to go home, I saw my dad at the end of the jetty, admiring my courage to learn something new and see it through. Needless to say, we both beamed with pride.

When I started Drexel University as an engineering student at age 26 with two pre-schoolers to care for and a husband also enrolled in school, failure was never a thought or an option. We sold everything, quit two jobs and returned to school. Would I have had the courage to start my career over as an engineer without the courage my father instilled in me as a girl? Probably not.

During my first electrical engineering lab, I remember thinking that I really didn't know anything about circuits. Being the only woman in the class, I assumed that I would learn much from the men. As we broke into our lab groups to begin an experiment, I quickly discovered that no one else know anything about circuits either. So I picked up the lab book and constructed my first circuit. I graduated second in my class and had 11 job offers to chose from. It just goes to show, as my father often said, that anything is possible if you work hard and learn from failure, as well as from success. I remembered that as I received a 36 percent on my first chemistry test! But I eventually managed an A in that course as well.

In terms of leadership, my dad had indispensable advice: First, leaders must be humble. Humility requires the courage to say, "I don't know," and the willingness to learn from others throughout the organization, including those below you on the organizational chart. Second, leaders must be lifelong learners. A transformational leader must be open to change.

Creating high-performing teams that can produce something meaningful and useful is fun. In many careers, you shuffle papers or work on efforts so large that you never really get the satisfaction of seeing tangible results. Engineering offers more immediate rewards. You actually can see, feel and touch the product of your efforts. There is nothing more exciting to me in my work than visiting an assembly plant and seeing the cars and trucks come off the line or watching a stock car race with the winning team displaying the Ford Motor Company oval.

The lessons from my father on risk-taking, lifelong learning and creating high-performing teams have been invaluable throughout my life and career.

GEORGE STEVENS, JR.

GEORGE STEVENS, Jr. is the son of prominent American director/cinematographer George Stevens, who won the Academy Award for directing the film classics *Giant* and *A Place in the Sun.*

George, Jr. has been involved in the entertainment industry from the age of one – though not voluntarily. His father sent him to the Hal Roach studios for a close-up in the Our Gang comedy "Wild Poses." It was evidently a sentimental gesture on the part of the father, who'd gotten his start at the Roach Studios.

George, Jr. began his official career in entertainment after graduation from Occidental College. He worked with his father as an assistant on such productions as *Giant* (1956) and *The Diary of Anne Frank* (1959). In 1962, Stevens was appointed head of the United States Information Agency's motion picture division, where he supervised the assembly of the classic documentary *John F. Kennedy: Years of Lightning – Day of Drums* (1964).

From 1967 through 1979, he was in charge of the American Film Institute, the independent, non-profit organization responsible for the preservation and restoration of so many rare films of the Nitrate Era (1895-1950).

Stevens' 1984 documentary tribute to his father, *George Stevens: A Filmmaker's Journey,* brought to public attention several reels of rare

Technicolor footage shot by Stevens Sr. during the Allied Invasion of Europe (1944-45).

George Stevens, Jr. won an Emmy for his first significant non-documentary work, the TV miniseries *Separate but Equal* (1991), in which Sidney Poitier played Thurgood Marshall.

In 1978 he created the Kennedy Center Honors with Nick Vanoff, and has produced and co-written the show for the past 26 consecutive years. The Honors telecast has been honored with five Emmys for Outstanding Program as well as the Peabody Award for Outstanding Contribution to Television.

I went with my father to the Academy Awards in 1951. He had directed a picture called *A Place in the Sun* with Elizabeth Taylor and Montgomery Clift, and I sat next to him and he won the Oscar. It was tremendously exciting. While we were driving home, my mother and grandmother were in the back seat, my father was driving and I was in the front seat with him. The statuette was on the seat between us. I was 17 years old and pretty overwhelmed, and I think he thought I was too excited. He looked over at me and said, "We'll have a better idea what kind of a film this is in about 25 years."

This was before video and retrospectives, and he felt that work was not just for the year or the moment but, if it were well done, it would be around for a long time.

Some years later I found myself being the founder of the American Film Institute, which was really based on the test of time, the preservation of film, the training of film makers and all that encompasses. It was something my father held dear.

Respect for the audience was so important to him. He never felt that you talked down to the people who were watching the picture. The studios at the time were fond of saying that the average audience had the mentality of a 14-year-old. When he made *Shane,* he said that critics described some intellectual aspects to it, which were valid, but he said he thought he made the picture for a truck driver in Indiana – a guy who drives the highway all day, is not articulate, cannot express everything that occurs to him, but is perceptive and can feel and think. I thought that was a wonderful insight, and it has helped me with my work. I have made a practice of aspiring to do things of quality rather than guessing what the audience predilection of the hour is.

In 1960, I was 28 years old and directing Alfred Hitchcock television shows while also working with my father on *The Diary of Anne Frank* as an associate producer. We were also preparing for *The Greatest Story Ever Told,* which was his very ambitious picture on the life of Jesus. I had become his *de facto* partner.

At one point journalist Edward R. Murrow came to Los Angeles to meet with the people of the movie industry, and he and I happened to meet one another. I got a call the next day from Samuel Goldwyn, Jr., who told me Ed Murrow wondered if I could come over the next day and spend an hour with him.

I said, "May I ask why?"

And he replied, "He's looking for someone to run the Motion Picture division of USIA." I told him I would love to spend an hour with Edward R. Murrow, but I would be wasting his time because I had committed to my father and we are doing everything together now. Goldwyn said okay and hung up.

An hour later he called back and told me Ed said I would not be wasting his time and to come up to Goldwyn's father's house the next day at 2:00 p.m. I went over and met with Murrow and it was enthralling and he was so impressive, and before long he offered me the job. But I gave him the same answer I had given Sam. Then we said goodbye and he told me that if anything changed to call him.

A couple of days later I was with my father over at 20th Century Fox, and we were talking about our different projects and somehow Murrow's name came up, and I mentioned I had met him. Dad asked why and I told him. And he said that I had to take the job. It was the generosity of a father who, though it made his very difficult project even more difficult, effectively losing one arm of support, knew how important it was for me to seek a newer world and have a chance to do something apart from his imposing reputation.

Obviously, I had great affection for him.

PAT SUMMITT

As the nation's winningest collegiate women's basketball coach completed her 30th season at the University of Tennessee, **PAT SUMMITT** reached yet another career milestone – coaching in more than 1,000 career games.

The 52-year-old head coach, who took over the reins of the program as a 22-year-old, eclipsed the 800-career-wins plateau midway through her 29th season on Jan.14, 2003. In doing so, she became the first woman in all of NCAA Division I basketball to accomplish such a lofty goal.

During Summitt's 30-year career at UT, she has helped dozens of women attain personal and team goals, including six NCAA titles, 22 Southeastern Conference tournament and regular-season championships, 11 Olympians, 17 Kodak All-Americans named to 29 teams, and 56 All-SEC performers.

At the 2000 ESPYs, her Lady Vols were chosen as "Team of the Decade."

Summitt is the author and subject of books, including *Reach For the Summit*, a motivational publication released in 1998 which made numerous best-seller lists, and *Raise the Roof,* a book that recapped the undefeated 1998 season released in October of 1998.

Patricia Head Summitt was born June 14, 1952, and graduated from UT-Martin in 1974. She received an M.S. in physical education from UT-Knoxville in 1975. She is married to R.B. Summitt and has one son, Ross Tyler Summitt, born September 21, 1990. They make their home in Knoxville along the banks of the Tennessee River.

It was really my dad who challenged and inspired me.

I have no regrets about my childhood because of what my dad taught me. I have three older brothers and a younger sister. I was the first daughter and treated like the fourth son. We were first and foremost taught the value of family, and we were always together as a family. We visited our grandparents on both sides, and our relatives were our friends and our support. It was all about family.

After family, our life was made up of church and school and work. I did not miss a day of school in my first 12 years. We were in church every Sunday, school every weekday, and worked on Saturday – but never on Sunday. "No job is too big or too small" was always the belief, along with "Hard work never killed anyone" (although there were a few days when I thought I was going to die). We had chores every afternoon doing things like milking the cows and helping my mom with our huge garden. We would freeze corn and can green beans. We made our own tomato juice, and all that we ate we had harvested ourselves.

My dad has a very strong character. He has never compromised his principles regardless of the situation. Without question, he is incredibly honest. He wants only what is his.

My dad is also a strong disciplinarian. He is a man with an incredible drive to be successful and a work ethic second to none. He started from scratch. He went out on his own and got a loan to buy his first farm by convincing the man at the bank that he was a hard worker and had a talent for farming. He was a man who was even more talented than *I* had realized. He turned that loan into a dairy farm, but we also had all the crops. We had corn and tobacco, and raised chickens, beef cattle and hogs. You name it and he did it.

Then he got into construction – building houses with his brother-in-law. Our town of 101 grew to many times that size, and my father was there to build the people their homes, and places for their businesses and a church. So when I look back and I think about my dad, I think of a man with incredible discipline and work ethic to do what he did and as successfully as he managed to do it.

He is incredibly generous. There is no telling how much money, to this day, people owe him; eventually we moved off the farm, he went into the grocery store business, then a hardware store, then we had a barber shop and a beauty shop – he built all this. But he was so giving and caring that he never asked for money from those he did not think could afford it.

His nickname was "Tall Man," and some people were afraid of him. He is a very opinionated man, whether it is politically speaking or speaking up in church or how he wants to conduct his business. But when you got to know him, he was just a teddy bear and would give you the shirt off his back – almost to a fault, at times.

There is a lot of my dad in my coaching. I often say I have a little of my mom but a lot of my dad.

One way I see my father in my style is exemplified in this story: As a young girl he took me out to the hayfield to rake hay, and I had never done it before. I had ridden on the tractor with my brothers and been around it but never tried it myself. So when I told him I did not know what to do, he said, "You won't learn any younger," and he let me out of the truck and I got on the tractor. He came back two hours later and I had figured it out. I think that in coaching you want players to take ownership and to give them responsibility, and then just let them go do it. A lot of times it is trial and error.

The way he encouraged accountability and responsibility within the family translates in coaching, and I talk a lot about those characteristics within the team dynamic. In many ways the team is like a family, and I try to develop that feeling to help develop a cohesiveness with the players. They need to be accountable and responsible to each other.

Being respectful is so important to me. We never disrespected our parents. Whether it was out of fear or love, we just grew up knowing they were our parents and deserved respect. I see a lot of that in our program, and we try to develop it on a number of levels. However, in one way it hindered me and it taught me to go in another direction, namely with communication. I did not have as great a give-and-take with him as I would have wanted. I was a little more fearful of him, but through that I learned, as a coach, the value of communication and the value of having the one-on-one with my players. My dad went so hard and fast and he was always working. I learned from my own experiences the importance of communication and developing relationships.

My dad taught me without being vocal about it. He would give me something to do and I would go do it. Now, when I give my son Tyler something to do, I will explain how it should be done and, right or wrong, it is still giving him responsibility. Communication is something that I wanted to be able to enhance between my son and me. It is almost like fast forwarding to the relationship I now have with my father. I have truly learned from our relationship, both past and present, and used it with Tyler.

I tend to treat my own son the way my father treated me in terms of expectations. I expect a lot from Tyler, but at the same time I think back about how, had I not been a coach, I probably would be able to spend more time with him, coaching and teaching him.

My father tried to coach my teams early on, and that was one of the first times I stood up to him. I just told him, "Dad, do not try to tell me how to coach. I am doing the best I can do, and I do not need a lot of people trying to help me. I have plenty of people who want to."

He has been so great with the success I have achieved. In 1996, when we came to Charlotte for the Final Four, my greatest hope was that he would be able to see us win the championship. He had not been able to see our previous championships in person, and I wanted it about as much for him as I did for the team. I knew what he had meant to the person and the coach I had become.

After the championship game, which we won, he gave me a big hug. There were tears running down his cheeks, which I had never seen with my dad. They were tears of joy, and he turned to me with wet cheeks and a big smile and said, "Somebody knows how to coach. I don't know whether it is Nikki, Holly or Al" (my three assistant coaches). It was his way of telling me he was proud of me, and I knew what he meant.

People have always respected my father and still do for a number of reasons. He was a strong father and family man, he is at church when the doors open, he has helped grow his church to a very sizable congregation and has built a good portion of the town in which we grew up. Everything that he has been associated with has been made better because of his input, and I think the community realizes it.

In short, he is a "difference maker."

ERIK WEIHENMAYER

Despite losing his vision at the age of 13, **ERIK WEIHENMAYER** has become one of the most celebrated and accomplished athletes in the world. Re-defining what it means to be blind, Erik has opened up the minds of people around the world. He has never let his blindness interfere with his passion for an exhilarating and fulfilling life.

On May 25, 2001, Erik became the first blind climber in history to reach the summit of Mt. Everest, the world's highest mountain. One year later, at the age of 33, Erik became one of fewer than 100 mountaineers worldwide to climb all of the Seven Summits – the highest peaks on each of the seven continents. He completed this incredible accomplishment on September 5, 2002, when he stood on top of Mt. Kosciusko in Australia.

Erik is a former middle school teacher and wrestling coach who has made his way onto the cover of *Time, Outside* and *Climbing* magazines. He has also been featured on the *Oprah Winfrey Show, NBC's Today,* the *Tonight Show* and *Nightly News with Tom Brokaw.*

In addition to being a world-class athlete, Erik is the author of the best selling book *Touch the Top of the World.* He is the recipient of numerous awards, among them the prestigious Freedom Foundation's Free Spirit Award and the 2002 ESPY award, and is the national spokesman for several literacy programs. Most of all, he is a proud husband and father to his four-year-old daughter, Emma.

Because my dad has done so well in business and in so many other pursuits, in many cases against the odds, I asked him one time, "Why are you so successful? I'm not trying to insult you, but it's not like you are smarter than other people." He responded in words I will never forget. He told me, "It is targeted perception." I thought that was super cool. Sometimes that can get you in trouble, because if your perception is too targeted you can miss out on a lot of things in life, like your family and so forth. But it is completely true – you just have to target something and stay focused.

When I was on Everest, I had made it through the Khumbu Icefall, which is a really, really difficult section of the mountain. It is basically jumbled up ice boulders of every size that are rolling and shifting under your feet, with huge drop-offs and crevasses everywhere. In short, it is not Americans-with-Disabilities-Act approved. It is a total nightmare for a blind person. The first time, it took me a miserable 13 hours. I was so wasted and thought, if it gets any harder, I don't know if I'll be able to climb this mountain. But I remembered a really insightful Tibetan quote: "The nature of the mind is like water. If you do not disturb it, it will become clear." I loved that and hung onto it, because so often when you think of something visionary or put a big goal out there for yourself, all the work, all the sacrifice, the risk and effort and all the potential for failure that lies ahead take away your will. In so many instances what beats you is an undisciplined mind. It was just another way of expressing my father's "targeted perception."

I have a young daughter named Emma who is only four. At this age, spending time with your kids is so important. It is not like I'm instilling any big complicated principles in her yet. I'm not telling her to keep her head up after striking out in softball or giving her social advice. That day will come soon. But I honestly believe that you teach a child at that age to trust people, to have a good foundation of security and confidence and hope. Tell them that things do work out in the end. It is certainly my responsibility to nurture her and blanket her with love, but also to set an example. Parents pass on to children an assortment of skills, leadership and courage. We do it through our words, through our constant nudging, but most powerfully through our actions. We must live the principles we hope to pass on, allow them to exude through our every decision, so that when Emma is ready to be passed the baton, and it is her turn to nudge and steer her own child, she'll be ready.

You do a lot of things in life that are very selfish. Climbing Everest and the Seven Summits was very personally gratifying for me. I do not do these things to prove that blind people can do them; I climb and do the things I do because I enjoy them. It is exciting. It is pioneering. But there is a bit of selfishness to it. It takes a lot of time away from my family. But more and more I have wanted to take my love of climbing and pass it on to other people, in effect, giving something back.

My dad gets a kick out of what I am doing and helps organize my schedule and stays on top of our projects. He is my biggest fan...and he is always full of ideas. Oftentimes he will come to me with a dream, and I'll laugh and say there is no way it is going to happen. But time goes by and eventually it does.

Just as I was climbing Everest, my dad e-mailed the editor of *Time* magazine about a possible feature. I told him, "Dad, c'mon, that guy gets a million e-mails like this a year. He is not going to care about me and my summit." Well, somehow, *Time* took notice, and my dad persistently followed up with dramatic Everest updates, even suggesting it would be an exciting cover story. Before we knew it, *Time* had dispatched a reporter to Nepal to cover the story. And then, unbelievably, I was on the cover of *Time*! That is a wonderful learning experience, because so many ideas are a long shot, but if you focus on them, stay on plan and remain stubborn, more times than you expect you can make them happen.

My father is a patriot and he passed his patriotism on to me, albeit with a twist. It was easier for people like my dad, who grew up in an era when fathers fought in World War II, when the war was drawn in such black and white terms. It was a simple case of good versus evil. Today it has become more difficult, with many shades of gray.

It's hard today to throw yourself into supporting things because they often seem so complicated. Patriotism seems so much more complex in 2005 than in 1945. My dad sees things in black and white, and believes in trusting our elected leaders to do what is right for the country, and in presenting a united front to the world. For me, though, it is hard not to question, but I am just as much a patriot and an American.

He was an attack pilot in the Vietnam War. He flew a ton of missions. He was there during what they call the good part of the war, at the beginning, before the protests, before it got too ugly.

In 1997 a non-profit group called World TEAM Sports organized a bike adventure in which I participated. Diverse teams of disabled and able-bodied folks biked together to show the power of teamwork. There is always a public education element in everything WTS does. This project was to ride the length of Vietnam– 1,200 miles north to south, Hanoi to Ho Cho Minh City (Saigon) on Highway 1. I rode on a tandem bike with my dad.

There were veterans from both sides of the war, both Vietnamese and Americans. Many of them were on hand cycles – double leg amputees and paraplegics – and there were blinded veterans as well. I laughed because I am blind and my father is a veteran, so when we rode together we were a "disabled veteran."

Halfway through the Vietnam Challenge, my dad and I pedaled our tandem towards the Hai Van Pass, rising 3,280 feet out of the coastal plains and separating former North Vietnam from South. The pass had a ten percent pitch that ran for six miles – the most physically demanding part of the ride. On this day we would need to be a team. My father had been the captain of the Princeton football team. He admitted that he wasn't the best athlete, but perhaps he was the most "enthusiastic." My dad loves a challenge, and he was going to get one on the Hai Van Pass.

The road rose gradually for awhile but then became

progressively steeper. As I pedaled, I couldn't stop thinking about the sound of my father's choking tears heard only the day before. I had heard him cry twice in my life, once when his father died and again after the death of my mother. But there he was, standing in the parking lot of the My Lai War Crimes Museum, the hot tears rolling down and burning his proud face. He said. "I had a friend," his words coming in concentrated bursts. "He got married to the same woman three times. They kept splitting up and then getting married again. His tour was done, after well over a hundred dangerous missions. He was going home, but on his last day he volunteered for one more flight." Dad took a deep breath. "His plane was lost somewhere over Vietnam. How can I believe that he died for nothing? I'm not proud of any war," he said softly, "but I am proud of my service to my country."

Listening to him against a backdrop of the Vietnamese anthem piped out over loudspeakers, I was beginning to understand that, for my father, patriotism was inextricably linked to the meaning of his own life. I awkwardly reached out my hand and touched his shoulder, and it was as though I was tenuously stepping out of one role and into another, because in the past, it had always been my father putting his hand on my shoulder.

After climbing the pass, at our last team dinner, Diana Nyad, the world's greatest long-distance swimmer, shared a conversation she had had with my father. She had used it for inspiration to guide her own life. "I have lived through a war," my father had told her. "I watched my son go blind. I saw my wife die in a car accident. By forging on, some people think I'm unfeeling. But what am I supposed to do? How am I supposed to act? Should I have given up? Should I have quit? Life is too precious, and all I can do is live it."

As I listened to Diana share my dad's words, I felt like I was emerging from a long dream. For almost three weeks now, I had been connected to my father by the frame of a tandem bike, but I hadn't always been connected to his story. I had struggled with my own blindness and with the crushing sadness of my mother's death. Like my father, I had chosen to live. In that way, I thought, my father and I were the same. Sitting at the dinner, reflecting on our bike ride through Vietnam, I was proud of my father, proud of myself, but especially proud to be my father's son.

BOB WEIR

As a founding member of The Grateful Dead, considered the most popular live act of all time, **BOB WEIR** was on the cutting edge of the counter culture and turbulent times of the 1960s and '70s. He and his fellow band members created a new genre in rock 'n' roll that has since been entitled "jam bands" and whose tradition has been carried on by acts such as Phish, Widespread Panic and the Dave Matthews Band. The group acted as both pied pipers and soundtrack to countless lives of individuals simply known as "Dead Heads" who followed them from show to show, in some cases for years on end. In 1995, after close to three decades on the road, the Grateful Dead came to an abrupt halt with the untimely death of band mate Jerry Garcia.

Weir's songwriting, musical contributions and touring continue with the surviving members of the band, who have recently reunited as The Dead. They continue to pack arenas all over the United States. Weir also fronts the band RatDog. He lives outside San Francisco with his wife Natascha and their two children.

Both my natural and adopted fathers were military men. My adopted dad attended Annapolis for seven years and came out with the military equivalent of a doctorate in engineering. When they gave him his first commission and put him out to sea, he was seasick from the time he left port to the time he got back. It was so bad they had to put him in the hospital. Then he tried it again right at the beginning of World War II. He wanted nothing more than to serve his country, but it just was not going to happen. He showed a lot of perseverance.

He was quite a guy. In fact, never in my presence did he ever use foul language. Rarely did I see him become angry. It was not that he wasn't a lively, energized person, but he was just a consummate gentleman. He was born with three kidneys, so he could drink all he wanted and was never affected. He did not drink much, but as far as getting a little buzzed, it was not a doable deal for him. I think one time my parents had a party and he was drinking pretty much all night, and toward the end of the evening I may have seen a twinkle in his eye. That was about it.

My natural father was born and raised in the Tucson, Arizona area. He was 19 when he joined the Air Force, and they put him behind the wheel of a bomber. He later became a test pilot and rose to the rank of colonel.

My adopted parents passed on in 1971 from separate illnesses. My mom died on my dad's birthday, and a month later my dad died on my mom's birthday. So you don't argue with that kind of stuff.

About ten years later I came home from a tour, and it was my first night home and I was trying to sleep in. I had this very strange dream about my family home, my brother and a stillborn baby. At one point of the dream my brother and I were holding the baby and each other, and I was awakened suddenly by the phone ringing in real life. It was the Grateful Dead office calling to say, "There's a lady on the phone by the name of Phyllis who says she's your mother. Do you know anything about this?" Apparently she had known for some time who I was and had been keeping track of me but had never made contact.

I had actually done some research myself to try and find my birth mother, but she had pretty effectively covered her tracks. I went and met her the next day, but unfortunately we did not exactly hit it off – she had twelve other kids. So I could ascertain with a fair bit of ease that she didn't really need me in her life. But I kept in touch with her, called her on Mother's Day, and over time she gave me some information regarding my dad – his name and where she last saw him, which at that point had been more than 40 years.

The story was that when she got pregnant, she ran off to San Francisco without his knowing, birthed me, gave me up for adoption, and then came back but never let on that I existed. So he had no idea he had a son. When she told me who he was, I had a private investigator track him down. It took all of an hour for the PI to find him. As fate would have it, he was the Director of Operations at Hamilton Field, the local Air Force base in San Francisco. Because I am almost pathologically anti-authoritarian, I figured this would not go well for either of us. You can't get much more authoritarian than the commanding officer of a military base.

I just sat on the info for close to ten years. Finally I figured, this guy's not getting any younger; I guess I better just buck up and do this. But there was still some apprehension because I didn't know what I was going to find. If my dad was an asshole, what does that say about me? I just assumed that military officers chose that profession so they could boss people around. So I figured I had three choices for contact: I could write him a letter, but he might crumple it up and throw it away; I could go see him, but the last thing I wanted was for my first and only memory of my father to be watching him clutch his chest and fall over backwards; or I could phone him. I decided to call.

It was early evening the next day. I called and said, "I'm looking for John Parber."

He said, "That would be me."

I told him, "Well, I'm Robert Weir and I live in Mill Valley, and I've been doing some research and have dug up some information that may be of considerable interest to you. But first I have to ask you a question or two."

He replied, "OK."

So I continued. "My questions concern events that took place in Tucson about 50 years ago. Is it possible that you were romantically involved with a woman by the name of Phyllis?"

He said, "Well, yes."

"Sir," I said, "in that case there's a very strong likelihood that, even though I'm not sure how many children you may have, you could have one more than you know."

There was a long silence, and then he said, "The only Robert Weir I know is the guy that sings and plays with the Grateful Dead."

And I said, "Well, sir, that would be me."

So we arranged to meet the next day at a local restaurant which coincidentally was a favorite of both of ours. We hit it off immediately and have become very, very close.

We both share a singular inability to take anything seriously, or an ability to make light of pretty nearly any situation. The more time we spend together, the more similarities I see and realize that the apple does not fall far from the tree. And even though I didn't grow up with him, in many ways I am as much, if not more, like him than his other sons.

On a weekly basis my family and I have been going up and staying with my father in Novato, where he now lives. We stay over for a night, and each morning "Grandpa" cooks me and my family pancakes. Towards the beginning of this year, he and his wife Milena began to leave a guitar out that once belonged to their eldest son, who tragically died of spinal cancer some time ago. He had been a professional musician in a fairly successful band and had a collection of guitars when he died; his brothers divvied them up, but because nobody really wanted this one, it had been left behind with his parents. They pulled it out of the closet – it was in a funky old case – and it was just sitting in the corner of their home. I saw this case for a month or so before I finally took the bait and opened it up. Inside was this beat up old Telecaster with one pickup kind of sprung out of its moorings and broken up a little. So after looking at it for two or three weeks, I finally said, "Okay, I'll bite. Can I take this to rehearsal with me and have my roadie / tech guy fix it up?" They said, "We thought you'd never ask."

So I took it and he had it working in no time at all. And I plugged it into my rig (amplifier) at our first rehearsal for the tour. Now, I had not even picked up a Telecaster in years, let alone played one, but I started playing it, and from the first note it was obvious for me, for the band, for everyone that its characteristically tin sound really was perfect for our stuff. It became my "A" guitar.

After no one wanting this guitar, it fell out of the sky on me.

All of the family is really overjoyed at seeing a piece of their older brother and eldest son make it to the big stage.

The whole story is really a little bit of mysticism.

The lesson I learned from my new dad is confirming for me that fate follows in your footsteps, so you need to have faith in your path and live life with a sense of wonderment.

JODY WILLIAMS

JODY WILLIAMS received the Nobel Peace Prize in 1997 for her work to eliminate antipersonnel landmines. International organizer and activist, teacher and writer, Williams is an eloquent speaker on human rights and international law, the role of civil society in international diplomacy, and individual initiative in bringing about social change.

She is one of only ten women to have received the Nobel Peace Prize, and only the third woman from the U.S. She was the founding coordinator of the International Campaign to Ban Landmines (ICBL), which was formally launched in October of 1992. In that capacity, she has overseen the growth of the ICBL to more than 1,300 Non-Governmental Organizations (NGOs) in more than 85 countries and served as the chief strategist and spokesperson for the campaign.

Working in an unprecedented cooperative effort with governments, U.N. bodies and the International Committee of the Red Cross (ICRC), the ICBL achieved its goal of an international treaty banning anti-personal landmines during the diplomatic conference held in Oslo in September 1997. Williams now serves as Campaign Ambassador for the ICBL, speaking on its behalf all over the world. Prior to beginning the ICBL, Jody Williams worked for 11 years to build public awareness about U.S. policy toward Central America.

From 1986 to 1992, she developed and directed humanitarian

relief projects as the deputy director of the Los Angeles-based Medical Aid for El Salvador. In that capacity, she developed a network of hospitals in 20 cities across the U.S. that donated medical care to Salvadoran children wounded in the war in that country. From 1984 to 1986, she was co-coordinator of the Nicaragua-Honduras Education Project, leading fact-finding delegations to the region. Previously, she taught English as a Second Language (ESL) in Mexico, the United Kingdom and Washington, D.C.

Williams has a Master's degree in international relations from Johns Hopkins School of Advanced International Studies, a Master's degree in teaching Spanish and ESL from the School for International Training, and a Bachelor of Arts degree from the University of Vermont.

Dad. John. Johnny. J.C. Big John. Johnny B. Good. The Judge. My dad. Asked to write about what I have learned from my father, first all of these names and nicknames came to mind. I began to think of so many aspects of dad and experiences with him that I found myself sort of stuck and at a loss as to how to begin to put dad to paper.

And then my sister – my spiritual twin/best friend sister, MaryBeth – came to visit and I talked with her about this exercise. Without hesitation, the first thing Moo (one of *her* nicknames) said was, "From dad we got absolute clarity of character. We learned that you do the right thing, even when nobody else is looking."

"Right on, Moo!" I enthused. She so got it right that my writer's block was broken.

Dad was the oldest of eight children – born in the Depression. Mostly what he has known in life is work. He began working very, very young to help provide for his other siblings. I cannot think of a time that dad has not worked, worked hard and wanted to work hard. Because he grew up with very little in a hardscrabble town in the poorest of times in the United States, more than almost anyone I know he values family, work, commitment. And under his sometime-bluster is also one of the most compassionate people I know.

Dad came home from World War II drop-dead handsome in his Navy uniform, and my mother took one look at him and knew he was the man for her. Life has not always been easy, but they have now shared 58 years of married life. Their first son was born deaf – in a tiny town in rural Vermont with no facilities for dealing with such challenges. So, each Sunday dad and mom drove Steve to a school for the deaf hours and hours and hours away in Connecticut – at a time that pre-dated interstate highways – where he lived and went to school. And each Friday they drove down to bring him home for the weekend.

But when that distance from family proved too much of a heartbreak for my brother, dad sold his thriving grocery store and their first home and moved the family to a larger town in Vermont with a school for the deaf, where my brother could go to school and live at home. The transition to that new town and finding work was not easy on my father or our growing family. But he kept at it, often working at more than one job to make ends meet until he managed to buy another small business and another home for the family, which now consisted of five children. More than 40 years later, my parents and my brother Steve still live in that house.

Dad worked hard to try to make sure his family had things he never had – even his deaf son, who in adolescence developed a violent form of schizophrenia, and whose various challenges had a huge impact on our family. Dad offered us the opportunity for higher education – something he never had and always thirsted for. He has stood by each and every one of his children as we have each gone through our growing pains in figuring out who we are on this planet, even when he might not have always thought our choices were the best. Dad feels intense pride in what all of his children have accomplished in our very varied lives. That pride shows when people ask him if he is particularly proud of what I have accomplished by being recognized with the Nobel Peace Prize; his uniform answer is, "I am proud of all my children."

At a time when most men would have retired, dad decided to take on something new, and with only a few weeks leading up to state primaries in Vermont, he managed to get his name on the ballot for the position of "Side Judge" (a lay advocate position to advise judges in civil cases in Vermont). He campaigned hard and won enough votes to unseat the incumbent. Dad gloried in the position, having the joy of exercising his intellect in ways that he would have had he been able to go to college. He continues working in the court to this day.

My father has taught me the value of hard work. He has taught me that family is there for each and every one us, no matter what. He has taught me to know who I am and to be comfortable with my opinions and have no fear of expressing them, no matter what others may think of them. From dad I learned the absolute necessity that your actions and your words mirror each other. Words are easy; the truth is told in the actions taken to back them up. His example has taught me to try to do the right thing always – even when nobody else is looking.

Dad. John. Johnny. J.C. Big John. Johnny B. Good. The Judge. My dad – he's mine and I love him.

John C. Williams died February 19, 2004, after suffering from cancer. My condolences and prayers go out to the entire Williams family.

ANDREW YOUNG

ANDREW JACKSON YOUNG, JR., born March 12, 1932 in New Orleans, Louisiana, is a great American politician, civil-rights leader and clergyman.

Young was reared in a middle-class family, attended segregated Southern schools, and later entered Howard University (Washington, D.C.) as a pre-med student to follow in the footsteps of his father, who was a dentist. He subsequently turned to the ministry and graduated in 1955 from the Hartford Theological Seminary in Hartford, Connecticut, with a divinity degree.

As a pastor at several black churches in the South, Young became active in the civil-rights movement – especially in voter registration drives. His work brought him in contact with Dr. Martin Luther King, Jr., and Young joined with King in leading the Southern Christian Leadership Conference (SCLC). Following King's assassination in 1968, Young worked with Ralph Abernathy until he resigned from the SCLC in 1970.

He was defeated that year in his first bid for a seat in Congress, but he ran again in 1972 and won. He was reelected in 1974 and 1976. He was an early supporter of Gov. Jimmy Carter, and after Carter's victory in the 1976 presidential election, Young was named the United States ambassador to the United Nations. He resigned in 1979. In 1981 Young was elected mayor of Atlanta, and he was reelected to that post in 1985, serving through 1989.

As a result of Young's visibility in both the national and international arenas, he was instrumental in bringing the 1996 Summer Olympic Games to Atlanta and served as Co-Chairman of the Atlanta Committee for the Olympic Games (ACOG).

President Clinton appointed him Chairman of the new Southern Africa Enterprise Development Fund (SAEDF). This $100 million fund helped to establish small- and medium-sized businesses throughout Southern Africa.

Young is a member of numerous boards, including Delta Airlines, Host Marriott Corporation, the Howard University Board of Trustees, the Georgia Tech Advisory Board, the Martin Luther King, Jr. Center Board of Directors, the Global Infrastructure Fund and the Center for Global Partnership.

Young has received many awards during his career, including the Presidential Medal of Freedom, America's highest civilian award; the *Legion d'Honneur* (France); and more than 35 honorary degrees from universities such as Notre Dame, Yale, Morehouse and Emory.

My father was a dentist and was always at home. His office was at the front of our house. My earliest recollection is whenever I would run through the office, he would stop me and make me go around and speak to all his patients.

My other memory is that he was a baseball player, and whenever he had a moment we would get a ball and play some catch.

When he was going to dental school, he and his friends earned their way by waiting tables up in the Catskills. Every one of the resorts had a baseball team, and if you were playing and hitting well, you would get the good tables and the good jobs. If you were in a slump, you would end up in the kitchen washing dishes. He really loved baseball.

He was a very thoughtful person and prepared us at a very young age to deal with racism. I grew up in New Orleans on Cleveland Avenue. On an opposite corner was an Irish grocery store, down the street was an Italian bar and 50 yards from our house I could hear people singing songs to Deutschland and shouting "*Hiel Hitler*." He explained racism to me by taking me to the movies to see the 1936 Olympic Games on the newsreels, where Jesse Owens was refuting, by his actions, the doctrine of Adolf Hitler. He used that lesson to help me see that I had no reason to fear that I was inferior to anybody, even though I was living in a neighborhood where we were officially second-class citizens. We did not play together in the streets with white kids, we had to go to different schools and there were always tensions with somebody calling us "nigger." He always said we should not get upset with those people because they are just ignorant and do not know any better. Don't get mad, get smart. If you lose your temper in a fight, you lose the fight. You need to fight with your head.

One day I went to the grocery store that was about four blocks away. I paid with ten dollars but they gave me change back for $20.

When I came home and bragged about it to my father, he said, "And you didn't correct their mistake?"

I said "No, that was their fault."

And he told me, "You run back, don't walk back, and apologize for not pointing out the error."

His honesty was not just something he preached. One day when I was about eight years old, the family was going to a movie. Although we lived in an integrated neighborhood, we had to go to a segregated movie theater. My father was driving and slowed down at a stop sign, but instead of coming to a complete stop, he eased through it and a policeman stopped him.

The policeman asked if he knew what he had done, and my father said, "Yes, I saw there was nothing coming and I did not come to a complete stop. I just went from third gear to second and kept on going."

The cop saw that his license said doctor, and he asked, "Well, Doctor Young, are you headed to an emergency? Were you going to the hospital to see a patient?"

My father said, "No, I was just taking my family to a movie." The police officer gave him every excuse to lie or even stretch the truth, but he would not do it. The policeman wound up not giving him a ticket. My mother, on the other hand, told my father he could have said he was on the way to see a patient, and he replied, "Yes, I could have, but I was not on the way to see a patient."

He said there are very few things in life that you can control totally, but one of them is your word, and it is one of the things that you cannot let anyone take from you. So I grew up that way. When I did something wrong, I admitted it and took the punishment, even when I did not think it was right. It was how I was taught.

There were six students from Louisiana that my father grew up with and went to college with. They played ball together in the Catskills and they also sang together. My father had a very good tenor voice and he loved to sing all the time. He sang in the choir, and every time the church door opened, we would have to be there because he was singing.

He was very proud that he had never once had a cigarette in his mouth and that he never drank. We had liquor in the house and he would ask me, when he was fixing a drink for someone else, if I would like a taste. Well, if you taste it as a boy, you do not like it. It is my one virtue that I have never had a cigarette in my mouth either. When I went to college and joined a fraternity, they said I could not get in the fraternity unless I smoked a pack of cigarettes and drank a pint of liquor. So I told them I would not join. They ended up harassing, hazing and roughing me up a little because of it, but I learned to stand my ground.

Father had a very rigid sense of Judeo-Christian values. Our church, the Congregational Christian Church, was one of the more liberal churches and remains so today. We were probably the first to recognize gay clergy and the first to ordain women. It had come south after the Civil War as part of the anti-slavery movement.

Ours was not a pious, self-righteous Christianity. The way my father expressed his Christianity was in what he did for others. The only thing that they quoted to me all the time was, "To whom much has been given, of them will much be required."

I went to Sunday school. My mother was the superintendent and was probably the most religious. We always said grace at meals, even when we were eating out at a restaurant. It did not make a difference. When I was eleven, my father went back to his class reunion at Howard University and took us with him. We were eating in a restaurant and we said the blessing, and the waitress told us she had been there for a long time but had never seen anybody pray in the restaurant.

Father used to try to get me to read everything – we had a lot of books. He gave me, when I was about 12, Wendell Wilkie's *One World.* I also had an encyclopedia from the time I was five or six. He was always encouraging me to read but it did not come easy to me. In fact, to this day I read with a highlighter, but I read constantly. Reading was part of our growing up in New Orleans. It was a rainy place, and if my brother and I began fussing and fighting with each other, my dad would say in a very serious tone, "Get a book! Sit down and read."

The one thing my father knew he wanted to do for us, because his father could not for him, was pay our way through college. He felt it was his responsibility to pay for our school and, if they could afford it, to give us a down payment on our first home. I have been able to do that with all four of my children as well.

My family ties were very strong. We made a big deal about sitting down at the table and eating together. We may not have done it for every meal, but at least once a day everyone sat down and ate at the same time.

Dad loved great speakers. He was very fond of Winston Churchill, Roosevelt and the great preachers like Gardner, who came to New Orleans when he was a young preacher. My parents took us any time there was anyone black in town who was important. Whether it was a lecturer or a singer or a concert pianist, we had to be there. It gave me a chance to see and meet people like the esteemed scholar, athlete, musician and actor Paul Robeson and the great litigator and future Supreme Court Justice Thurgood Marshall.

My father always taught me, and I understood from a very young age, that our plight was very political even though there were not many black people voting. One time he told us, because he did not like us playing ball in the street, that there was an empty lot across the street we could use. When I told him that it was overgrown with weeds, he said that since it was almost time for an election, maybe I should call the city and ask them to come cut the grass. When I protested, saying that they would not come out for me, he said they did not know who I was, that I was simply a citizen asking for city services. I did call, they came out, and it was a lesson about politics that I never forgot.

My father used to say that you could not make it in this life if you are just as good as everybody else. You need to do it better than anybody else. Just as good is not enough.

He believed in absolutes. There is no such thing as 90 percent right or almost right. Either you are 100 percent right or 100 percent wrong. He had a very strong moral sensibility. We were rebuilding the church when I was a child, and my mother and father always contributed even though they really did not have any money other than what they were saving for our education. My mother was always proud that she did not have a fur coat, and we did not even have a car most of the time. Other black people in the professions took it for granted that you owned a car and a fur coat. But whenever the construction on the church was in danger of stopping, the minister would come by and my daddy would go into his savings. Mother would tell him he was robbing his children because the money was for our education, but building the church was part of my education and Dad thought it was 100 percent right.

He did not want me to be a minister. He really wanted me to be a dentist and play baseball. When I was sworn in as ambassador to the United Nations by Supreme Court Justice Thurgood Marshall, a man we had been taken to see speak so many years before, he said to my father, "You must be very proud of this boy."

My daddy's answer was, "If he would have been a dentist, he really would have been somebody."

A Lesson I Have Learned from My Father:

Father's Name: ______________________________

Father's Date of Birth: ______________________

Check out these other fine titles by
Durban House online or at your local book store.

Exceptional Books
by
Exceptional Writers

FICTION

BASHA	John Hamilton Lewis
CRY HAVOC	John Hamilton Lewis
SAMSARA	John Hamilton Lewis
HANDS OF VENGEANCE	Richard Sand
PRIVATE JUSTICE	Richard Sand
WATCHMAN WITH A HUNDRED EYES	Richard Sand
DEADLY ILLUSIONS	Chester Campbell
DESIGNED TO KILL	Chester Campbell
SECRET OF THE SCROLL	Chester Campbell
MEDUSA STRAIN	Chris Holmes
THE GARDEN OF EVIL	Chris Holmes
DANGER WITHIN	Mark Danielson
THE INNOCENT NEVER KNEW	Mark Danielson
HORIZON'S END	Andrew Lazarus
THE STREET OF FOUR WINDS	Andrew Lazarus
ALIBI ON ICE	Ben Small
THE SERIAL KILLER'S DIET BOOK	Kevin Mark Postupack
JOHNNIE RAY & MISS KILGALLEN	Bonnie Hearn Hill & Larry Hill

NONFICTION

AFTER SCHOOL CHATS (ADVICE FROM FATHERS TO THEIR SONS)	George Bradt
HELP!! (HOW TO FIND, HIRE, TRAIN & MAINTAIN YOUR HOUSEHOLD HELP)	Marta Perrone
JIM BOWIE (FRONTIER LEGENDS)	Robert Hollmann
LESSONS FROM OUR FATHERS	Keith McDermott
MOTHERS SPEAK... FOR LOVE OF FAMILY	Rosalie Fuscaldo Gaziano
PROTOCOL	Mary Jane McCaffree, Pauline Innis and Richard Sand
SEX, LIES AND P.I.'s	Ali Wirche, Marnie Milot
SPORES, PLAGUES, AND HISTORY – THE STORY OF ANTHRAX	Chris Holmes
THE MAN WHO FED THE WORLD	Leon Hesser
THE NAKED WRITER	G. Miki Hayden
THE PASSION OF AYN RAND'S CRITICS	James S. Valliant
WHAT MAKES A MARRIAGE WORK	Malcolm Mahr
WHITE WITCH DOCTOR	Dr. John A. Hunt

NONFICTION

AFTER SCHOOL CHATS (ADVICE FROM FATHERS TO THEIR SONS)	George Bradt
HELP!! (HOW TO FIND, HIRE, TRAIN & MAINTAIN YOUR HOUSEHOLD HELP)	Marta Perrone
JIM BOWIE (FRONTIER LEGENDS)	Robert Hollmann
LESSONS FROM OUR FATHERS	Keith McDermott
MOTHERS SPEAK... FOR LOVE OF FAMILY	Rosalie Fuscaldo Gaziano
PROTOCOL	Mary Jane McCaffree, Pauline Innis and Richard Sand
SEX, LIES AND P.I.'s	Ali Wirche, Marnie Milot
SPORES, PLAGUES, AND HISTORY – THE STORY OF ANTHRAX	Chris Holmes
THE MAN WHO FED THE WORLD	Leon Hesser
THE NAKED WRITER	G. Miki Hayden
THE PASSION OF AYN RAND'S CRITICS	James S. Valliant
WHAT MAKES A MARRIAGE WORK	Malcolm Mahr
WHITE WITCH DOCTOR	Dr. John A. Hunt